The Yards of Atherstone

The Friends of Atherstone Heritage

Recordings of their oral histories can be found on our website www.atherstonesheritage.com

Although this book has concentrated on the Atherstone yards the Atherstone Rural District Council also had responsibility for the yards in Hartshill, Polesworth and Baddesley Ensor and records of these are in Warwickshire County Record Office.

Printed and published on behalf of the Friends of Atherstone Heritage by:

AnchorPrint Group Ltd
Syston
Leicester
LE7 2LE

First published 2012

ISBN Number: 978-1-907540-58-5

The Yards of Atherstone

Research carried out by a group of volunteers based at the Volunteer Centre North Warwickshire.

Marion Alexander, David Ball, Eileen Barrs, Oliver Cartwright, Pam Colloff, Lorna Dirveiks, Lisa Hill, Martin Horner, Jean Jeffries, Alan Joynson, Amber Neat, Emma Sankey, Janet Stuart, Mike Trye, Jen Tudor.

Thanks are also due to the Volunteer Centre Staff who offered much valuable assistance in typing and proof-reading.

Thanks must also go to the many inhabitants of Atherstone who allowed themselves to be interviewed by our volunteers and who provided much useful information as to what life was like in earlier years.

This is an early aerial view of Atherstone showing the density of housing in the centre of town. The crossroads, bottom left, is where Coleshill Road, Station Street and South Street meet. The first clearance scheme was the Nelson Yard scheme, currently the Bus Station, just up from this crossroads.

Contents

References

Photographs of the yards from the collection held in the Warwickshire County Record Office together with other records held in their collections. Other photographs generously supplied by local people.

The old maps of Atherstone were based on the Ordnance Survey Warwickshire Sheet VI.II.23 Atherstone, First Edition 1881.

On-line Census data 1841 – 1911
The National Archives

Research information by Year 8 History group 2010-2011, Queen Elizabeth School and Sports College, Atherstone, Warwickshire.

Reference was also made to the following publications:

The History of Atherstone, Watts & Winyard
Hats, Coal & Bloodshed, Austin
Atherstone A Pleasantly Placed town, Alcock & Hughes
Once Upon a Time in Atherstone, Hughes

The Yards of Atherstone

Introduction

For most of the 19th century and much of the 20th century the majority of people in Atherstone lived in cramped 'one-up-one-down' houses built in the back yards of pubs, shops and dwellings. These cottages were built 'back-to-back' and very close together, why did they take this form in an otherwise green and rural area?

The development of Atherstone as a community

There has been a settlement in Atherstone since before the Romans came 2000 years ago. They drained and 'metalled' the ancient track we now call the Watling Street, making transporting people and goods easier and paving the way for Atherstone to become the centre of trade that it still is today.

Domesday Book records eleven villagers, two smallholders and one slave, as living in Atherstone in 1086. The families lived off the land and paid taxes, or tithes, to the landowners, in return a good landlord would promote and improve the town.

In 1375 the landowner was a French community of monks who built a small Friary near where St. Mary's Church still stands. There were 12 monks and their leader, the Abbott of Bec, had the ambition to make Atherstone a more prosperous place. He marked out thirteen and a half burgage plots around the Market Place and along Watling Street, hoping to attract free tenants who would bring prosperity to the town.

By the end of the century the number of burgages had risen to thirty-six. Charters were granted by the King for twice-weekly markets and a September fair, which developed into the annual 'Statutes' or hiring fair where labourers would seek employment for the coming year. Despite the Abbot's efforts, however, the town never achieved borough status, though its importance as a trading centre did increase.

A 'burgage plot' is a piece of land as wide as the frontage of the house and extending as far as the 'backway' (North Street or South Street) and it could be used to grow vegetables and to keep chickens and pigs. In addition every householder was allocated strips of land in the 3 big fields surrounding Atherstone so they could grow wheat and other grains. They also had the right to graze their sheep, cows and horses on the Outwoods and the Cow Pasture. A byelaw said that pigs had to be kept on the burgage plots because they grubbed up the turf on common land making it unusable to other animals.

There are few examples of these gardens left in the modern town except for the garden behind Old Bank House, which is currently (2012) open to the public on weekdays.

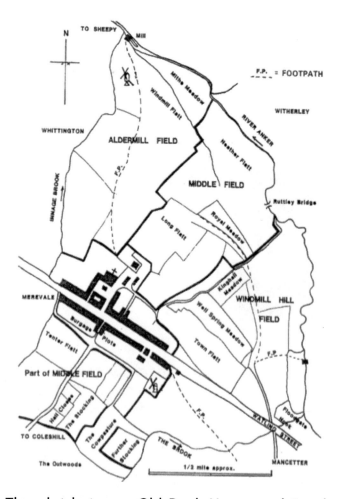

The plot between Old Bank House and South Street is still as it might have been when this plan was drawn up in 1716. The entry is large enough to take a horse-drawn carriage.

In 1613 Sir John Repington inherited the Manor of Atherstone and decided to live in the town and build himself a fine house. The first Atherstone Hall was completed in 1619. Sir John was a merchant, not a farmer, and he could see that farming strips with paths in between was wasteful of land. Later landowners saw the efficiency of owning land in fields, not in scattered strips. In 1735 an Agreement was drawn up to enclose the land.

The smaller cottagers united against enclosure because they feared they would get inferior land, they also feared losing their right to graze animals on the Outwoods. Horses were the only form of transport and carriers as well as farmers relied on their traditional rights to feed their animals on the common land.

This first attempt failed but in 1765 an Act of Enclosure was passed by which most of the land went to a few prominent citizens. However, the Outwoods, the Cow Pasture and the Clay Pits were not enclosed and this was confirmed in an act of 1784 in which 70 acres of the Outwoods was declared to be freehold property belonging to the people of Atherstone.

Prior to enclosure farming, along with other trades such as hatting, had been small scale and largely carried out as a way of providing for your family. Any surplus would be sold or bartered to obtain livestock or goods that you were unable to produce yourself. Steam power, the opening of the canal in 1790 and the coming of the railway 50 years later, collectively called the 'Industrial Revolution', saw manufacturing moving out of the cottages and into factories . The increased production could now be moved cheaply to London and abroad along the improved roads, the canals and the railways. Entrepreneurs started selling Atherstone hats, coal and granite to the world so more factories were built and more workers were needed. Most of these workers came from the countryside putting great pressure on the few houses in Atherstone. This happened all over England and in most places factory owners built rows of cottages in the fields round their new factories, but not in Atherstone because one result of enclosure was that two families owned most of the land North and South of Watling Street.

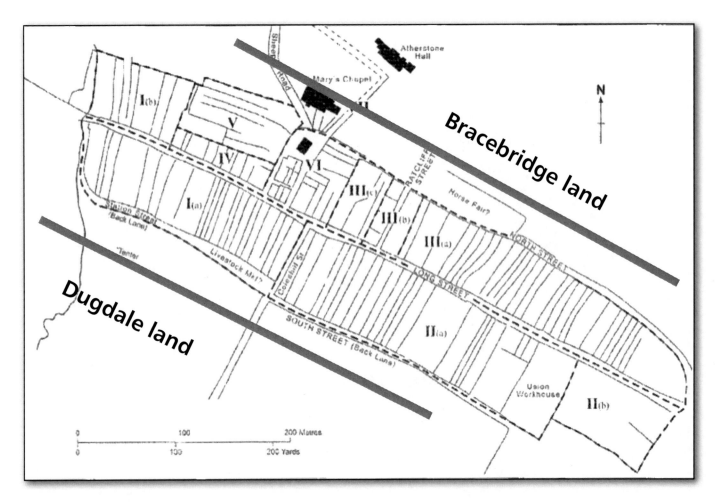

The map above shows how the Dugdale family owned most of the land beyond South Street surrounding Merevale Hall and the Bracebridges were similarly situated to the North owning all the land round Atherstone Hall (*now Windmill Road and Holte Road*). The only 'spare' land was in the plots owned by householders and called 'Burgage Plots'.

The rise of the Yards

From their inception householders had subdivided their burgage plots and sold off parts on which the new owner would build a house, stable or a workshop. So in 1736 a poor rate assessment lists 231 houses fronting on Long Street and the Market Place and '72 back tenements' usually small houses built at the far end of the plot, 303 households in all. The Land Tax Assessment for Poor Relief dated 1768 (WCRO CR258/482) lists every house in Atherstone. This assessment notes each owner or occupier of the front properties and indicates how many 'houses in the yard' there were. The names of occupiers of the yard houses are also given.

If this assessment is used in conjunction with the 1786 plan of the copyholders and freeholders in Atherstone on Long Street it has been possible to place the 52 positions of these 'houses in the yard' accurately on later maps. This information has been used in the detailed descriptions of the yards to identify when the yard was first known.

An 1801 survey of property in Atherstone recorded almost double that number of dwellings (556) of which Mr. Nuthall, a feltmonger, owned 24, and William Bingham, a grocer, owned 18. Benjamin Harris, a builder, let out 34 houses and Thomas Carver, the schoolmaster, had 13 to rent. A report 12 years later showed an increase of 22 houses and this frenzy of building continued until there were nearly 1000 houses in 1851 all built on the land between South Street (*Station Street*) and North Street (*Croft Road*). Such a rate of building shows that some inhabitants were prospering, men like John Vinrace, a wool stapler, who gave his name to Vinrace's Row and well-known Atherstone hatter, Joseph Wilday, who built Wilday's Terrace in the 1830s. By 1848 Avin's Yard, below, was typically full of mainly rented cottages.

Avins Yard looking towards Long Street circa 1910

These houses were built in haste and built very badly. In 2005 the land in Station Street was being cleared prior to the building of Aldi's supermarket. Archeologists were given access to the site and found very clear traces of individual yard homes in Cordingley's Yard and Bingham's Row. Nat Alcock in "Atherstone: A Pleasantly Placed Town" describes the findings on pages 186 and 187. He found that the houses were built directly onto the earth with no foundations and the dividing walls were only one brick thick. The floors were red brick often with quarry tiles on top with perhaps a rag rug or piece of lino covering the cold tiles. The houses varied in width from 11 feet (3.5m) to 16 feet (5m) and were about 15 feet (4.5m) deep. The front wall contained a window and a door leading directly off the yard into the living room with a fireplace on a side wall back-to-back with the fireplace in the next house. A partition in front of the back wall formed a small pantry and a boxed in stair with a coal-hole under the stairs.

Cordingley's Yard looking towards Long Street

This is Druids Arms Yard (the bus station at the back of Jeffcot's plant shop) showing washing drying and a lady cleaning her window

The yards themselves varied widely but, suffice it to say, that each yard, regardless of how many people lived in it, would have only one pump or tap, one or two 'privies' an ash-pit and an open drain running down the middle of the yard. Every day was washday because the one or two wash houses had to be used on a rota. The bath usually spent most of the week hanging on the wall outside until bath night when the whole family would bath in turn in front of the fire. Water for bathing or washing had to be first brought into the house in heavy buckets then heated on the open fire.

Individual Yards and their stories

Sometimes research reveals interesting human stories which can be authenticated from memories or photographs such as these two examples.

Garden Row 1841 – 1965 *No other name*

This was the last yard to be demolished to make room for the building of the Library, Clinic and Memorial Hall. Many Atherstone residents have fond memories of this yard and the feeling of community engendered by the families who lived there as shown by the decoration of the entrance to celebrate the Coronation of Queen Elizabeth II in 1953.

The Wills family are first recorded living at number 12 Garden Row in 1881 when Charles Wills Snr was recorded as living with his first wife, Louise. They had no children but shared their cottage with an eleven year old niece and two lodgers, one male, one female. The young lady lodger was a twenty year old hat machinist from Polesworth called Hannah Spooner, probably in Atherstone because of the availability of work and it was this girl who became Charles' second wife on the death of Louise later in 1881.

Charles and Hannah were to go on to have seven children in the little house in Garden Row one of whom was Charles Wills, the artist. Their first born in 1883 was called Louisa , probably in memory of her father's first wife, and she later married and became Louisa Jephcott. The next two children were girls, Mary and Edith who went on to become Mrs. Morris and Mrs. Allsopp. When Edith was three, Charles William, the only boy, was born on February 28th. 1891 and from the first there seems to have been a special bond between mother and son.

Three more girls were born, Harriet (later Chetwynd), Alice and Dorothy, unfortunately Alice died aged 10 months in 1898 but Dorothy, who never married, was to be the person who shared her home with Charles in his later years and who was responsible for passing on her brother's work after his death.

We know very little about the Wills' family life around the turn of the century but Atherstone was a thriving town with many hat factories, two weekly markets and a busy trade in livestock often through the railway station which in 1900 was busier than nearby Nuneaton. Garden Row was right in the middle of town, where the Library and Memorial Hall are now, and Mr. Wills earned a living by house painting and decorating. Hannah Wills, as well as looking after her family, did cleaning for money working at some time for the Bracebridge family at Atherstone Hall but she was also very active at St. Mary's Church in Atherstone's Market Place where she did the cleaning as her service to her church. Other members of the family also lived in Garden Row which had gardens in which they kept chickens and pigs. Charles Wills Snr. won a medal as the "most successful exhibitor"

Garden Row looking from Long Street

at Atherstone Horticultural Society Exhibition of 1894. His nephew, Mr. Morris of Mancetter Road, lived at no. 6 and remembers well his grandmother, Charles' mother, and her keen involvement with St. Mary's Church, Atherstone, because she used to take him, aged 5, with her when she went to the church to clean. He also remembers Uncle Charles very well because he was always getting him to sit for portraits and there are several examples of these owned by the artist's family.

Binghams Row

The Baddesley pit disaster of 1882 took the lives of 32 men most of whom lived around the mine at Baxterley and Baddesley.

Just 2 Atherstone men lost their lives and they both lived in Binghams Row (*the yard under the present Aldi shop*). This was the most over-crowded yard in the town with a population density greater than the most crowded of Birmingham's slum dwellings.

This shows Binghams Yard looking towards Station Street, it was also called Willdays Yard.

You can see a hat factory in the background with the tall boiler house chimney dominating the yard.

This photograph is of Emma Archer of Bingham's Row and her five children taken in 1885. (Thanks to Stan Archer)

Emma's husband, Richard, was one of the Atherstone men involved in the pit disaster and, although he was rescued alive and taken home, he finally succumbed to his injuries 2 months later, on June 29th 1882. Imagine nursing a man with severe burns in one of the tiny houses in Bingham's Row whilst looking after five children under the age of 11!

A quick look through the Census forms shows that Emma went on to marry William Archer, her husband's cousin, in 1883 and together they had Emma 1885, Maud 1888, Richard 1894, Alfred 1897 and Beatrice 1900 – a total of 10 children. In 1901 Emma and William had moved back to Grendon with eight of their children, the older ones having left home to work, Joseph living on a farm in Sheepy and William serving as a baker on Long Street, Atherstone.

Emma died in 1939 aged 86, three months after her husband, William. Sadly burial records also record that while she lived in Bingham's Row Emma lost 3 children in infancy.

The changing face of Industrial Atherstone

From medieval times until the 18th century Atherstone changed very little with families being self-sufficient by growing crops and keeping animals. Some townspeople would specialise in shoe-making, blacksmithing or tailoring to serve the inhabitants and those living in the villages around and there were several wind and water mills to turn grain into flour.

The town developed as an important market town where farmers exchanged or sold their produce. As wood was used up and not replanted it was replaced by coal from the area round Baddesley, which helped to develop industries in the town. As well as coal mining and farming the traditional industries were hat making, brewing of beer and soft drinks and tanning, all based on there being a good supply of fresh water. Four streams ran from the Hartshill ridge through Atherstone to the River Anker, this ridge was also the source of hard rock which had been mined since Roman days.

Atherstone was at the height of its prosperity near the end of the 19th Century. First the canal, then the railway had helped with trade. Atherstone was the centre for distributing post, first from the mail coaches then through the railway. A trades directory of 1870 lists 10 butchers, most of whom would have their own slaughterhouses. The town had a flourishing livestock market, its own Corn Exchange and was famous for its cheese market. Every year in September there was a 'Hiring Fair' where agricultural workers could be hired for the coming year from outside the Angel Inn where they stood holding a pitchfork or shearing clippers to indicate their specialisms.

Agriculture

Prior to World War II a farmer at Hurley would expect to feed 60 workers at harvest time and employ up to 20 people throughout the year. The war made farmers look to less people-intensive farming, substituting tractors for horses, as the skilled men and women were called up into the forces. Many of the inhabitants of the yards are listed as 'agricultural workers'

Hatting

Hat making had developed in Atherstone as a 'cottage industry'.The earliest felt caps were knitted in the round from yarn, then felted in troughs of fullers earth. This capping trade was carried on in Coventry from medieval times. Hatting spread to Atherstone in the 17th century. In 1672, Samuel Bracebridge, a "Haberdasher of Hats" (i.e. a merchant) was supplying materials to cottage feltmakers. Atherstone was well suited to the trade because of a plentiful supply of water and fuel.

In 1696 Joseph Hatton, feltmaker, wrote his will:

"In the Workhouse 2 poore old kettles & 3 Sorry Basons and Hattblooks & other old lumber" Valued at 9 shillings and 4 pence.

Before factories were built, felt hats were made in small workshops in the yards behind houses in the town. Using a 'feltmaker's bow', the feltmaker would produce a bundle of wool, termed a "batt". The batt was separated into two equal parts of a roughly triangular shape and pressed gently between a hurdle and a piece of leather. It was then taken to the "bason", an iron plate over a small hearth where the feltmaker pressed it, sprinkled water over it, and worked the wool gently so that it began to felt.

The two triangles were then folded together into a cone shape with a piece of cotton cloth inside to prevent the sides felting together. Using steam and pressure the men worked the felt form until it shrank to almost a third of its size. Next the felt hood was dried, stiffened and blocked. These processes would take place in attics and workshops tucked away behind the houses fronting Long Street.

Trimming was done by the women of the family, often outside on sunny days as most of the workers lived in the 'yards' where there was very little room indoors. By the 1790s a number of hatters workshops had become established in Atherstone and many families were moving into the town to work in the trade. A shortage of land was forcing the intensive development of the yards behind the houses. Narrow dwellings lined the yard and a hatters' workshop often stood at the far end.

The Entrepreneurs

Hatting in Atherstone was organised by five generations of the Bracebridge family. Cottage feltmakers collected wool from the Bracebridges, took it home and made it into hoods during the time they had to spare between tending their crops and their stock.

By the 1780s the Bracebridges had sold out to one of the most prosperous of the cottage feltmakers, John Wilday, who had taken an apprenticeship in London, and was also a banker. By this time specialised premises were developing. John Wilday's son, Joseph, set up the first purpose-built hatting factory in Atherstone in Wilday's Yard which also contained houses rented to the factory workers.. After Joseph Wilday died in 1852, the premises were leased by Hall and Phillips.

Charles Vero's family had been hatters in Atherstone since 1786. His brother-in-law, James Everitt, was the son of a tallow chandler with premises in central Long Street. The two men formed a partnership on the eve of a voyage to Australia in 1851, where they set up a hat shop in Melbourne.

In 1855 Charles Vero returned and rented from W.S. Dugdale a premises in the "South Backway" in Atherstone. Over the next fifty years, Vero & Everitt's factory expanded.

Machinery was introduced in the mid-nineteenth century, and Vero & Everitt filed several patents for improvements in the processes. Hats were exported all over the world from the factories built in the middle of the town.

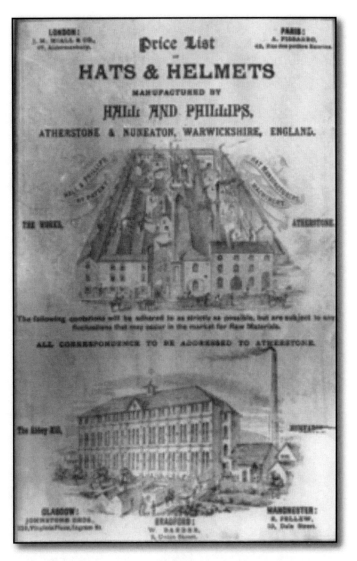

Hall & Phillips relocated to Nuneaton. However, by the early years of the 20th Century there were a number of substantial hat factories in Atherstone:

Denham & Hargrave, F.J. Elliott & Co.,

Thomas Townend & Co., W.A. Hatton Ltd

Vero & Everitt Ltd and Wilson & Stafford Ltd.

In 1986 only three remained:

Austin Aspden Ltd   Vero & Everitt Ltd

Wilson & Stafford Ltd.

Feltmaking in Atherstone ceased in March 1999, when Wilson & Stafford went into liquidation. Vero & Everitt Ltd continued to manufacture a small number of uniform hats in the town until the site was sold to ALDI. Several empty factories still remain in the town, a reminder of the industry that gave Atherstone its identity and pride.

Coal mining

The Romans burnt coal 2000 years ago and the monks at Merevale Abbey left coal ash, but it was not until the 16th Century that people started to burn coal to heat their homes, to melt iron and in the manufacture of glass and lime.

At places like Baddesley Common where the coal occurred on the surface, families dug into the seam and carried the coal away, digging along the measure and forming a drift mine.

Sometimes they dug out the coal until a large bell-shaped chamber was left which would then collapse inwards if it was not propped up by timber.

With the Industrial Revolution of the 18th. Century the demand for coal increased and prospectors spent large amounts of money establishing the extent of the Warwickshire Coalfield which they found went from Tamworth to Coventry where the coal seams joined to make a seam 24 feet thick.

The mine at Baxterley about 1882

Although there is no coal under Atherstone, mining was a major employer in the town for over 100 years. The pit at Baddesley was first sunk by the Dugdale family of Merevale Hall in 1850. Apart from a set-back in 1882 when there was a disastrous accident (*see aol.hometown, Baddesley/Baxterley Pit Explosion 1st - 2nd May 1882*) it was a profitable pit when it was nationalised in 1948. It finally closed in 1989,

Government Census reports show large numbers of Atherstone men earning a living from mining. A typical entry in the 1891 Census showed that Nelson's Yard in Atherstone (*now the Bus Station*) had 12 houses.

Colliers families lived in 3, a similar number earned a living in hatting and there were 3 agricultural workers.

Mineral water manufacture

A little known industry which was important to the town of Atherstone was that of mineral water manufacturing. Nowadays there are no traces of the factories that mixed and bottled 'pop' but we know from the bottles that can still be excavated from Victorian rubbish dumps that there were dozens of small enterprises bottling mineral waters and proudly displaying their embossed names on their bottles. Many of the firms were connected to public houses and were in the sheds in the yards off Long Street or round Atherstone's Market Place. The oldest container found so far is a flagon and has the name Ann Beech, Atherstone, printed on it. Pigot's trade directory of 1828 records that Ann Beech was a Chemist and Druggist with a shop in Atherstone Market Place. Later, in the same directory of 1862, she is described as being a Grocer and Tea Dealer still in the Market Place. Both chemists and grocers are known to have bottled their own soft drinks, Ann seems to have done so for over 40 years.

Ann's son Joseph took over the shop because, as with Atherstone's other great industries, coal mining and hat making, children tended to follow their parents into the industry. The Fielders, the Chetwynds, the Barnsleys and the Hiornses are named as running businesses for many years, As is to be expected, many of these pop makers were also publicans and, as with the hatting families, their names crop up on committees and charities as they helped to run the town.

A selection of Atherstone 'Codd' bottles collected by Alan Jones

Freeman, Morgan and Albrighton are all names associated with lemonade making around the year 1900; in fact Albrighton's address in 1899 was 'The Aerated Waterworks' Atherstone.

One lemonade name that has stuck in Atherstone is 'Barnsley'. The cut-through from Long Street to Aldi's is called "Barnsley Court" from the days when John C Barnsley set up a factory in the yard behind the shops.

Hiorns bottling plant 1930s

The name Hiorns was connected to the licensed trade as far back as 1872 but Hiorns Brothers, who had a factory in Meadow Street and a bottling plant in Little Grove Road, were first listed in Kelly's Directory of 1912. They continued to produce and bottle mineral water until the late 1960s or early 70s. Mr. Caswell, the last manager of the last mineral water firm, lived in the bungalow on Little Grove Road and was universally known as 'Charley Pop'. He would tell you about the secret recipes for 'Tizer' and other delights he had locked in his safe. When the firm was bought out, he retired and the bungalow was sold for housing. (*The Orchard*)

Other trades

It is difficult to know how many trades were carried out actually in the yards as the census only records trades and the trade directories tend to give the location as Long Street, Station Street etc. even when it is known that the workshop was 'up a yard'. Within modern memory there was a blacksmith in Phoenix Yard in Church Street and there are several blacksmiths listed in censuses as living in yards. It is much more likely that they shod horses in a yard rather than on Long Street, particularly as we know from contemporary writing that many, if not most, yards contained stables.

For example, the Warwickshire Trade Directory of 1861 lists 161 trades as being in Long Street or the Market Place. There were 27 shopkeepers, 37 public house keepers, 16 grocers, 6 drapers, 4 bakers and 10 butchers, a total of 100 businesses in a town with only 1000 buildings. Of the 61 remaining 17 were boot and shoe makers, 19 hat or bonnet makers and 5 seamstresses, all of whom may have had shops on the main street but who, equally, might have traded from their homes in the yards. Other trades included in the directory are 3 hairdressers, a chimney sweep, 3 builders and an architect, 3 bookseller/printers, 3 saddlers, 2 photographers and the same number of watchmakers with one ironmonger, a tinplate worker, a nailmaker and one firm selling lamp oil.

Atherstone was a flourishing market town with all the trades needed for a comfortable life. Although there were unemployed people (paupers) in the Workhouse and the yards, there were enough people with money to support shops selling high class luxury goods.

Equally there was enough poverty to require a pawnbrokers shop, complete with a discreet hatch hidden from view up the alley leading to Nelsons Yard.

Incidentally this is the last entry permanently open to the public and designated a 'Right of Way'. Walking through, it is easy to imagine mothers struggling along carrying shopping and babies, the whole family bucketing Dad's coal allowance from the pit and, at night, the 'night soil men' slopping through the alley carry a large bucket of human waste out to the cart on Long Street.

Life in Atherstone from contemporary sources

Pre-WWII

There are very few written accounts of 19th century Atherstone, however, we have been able to use some documents kept in the Warwickshire County Records Office and others owned by local families through which we have been able to build up a picture of life in the yards when they were at their highest rate of occupancy.

Phoebe Sheavyn was born in Atherstone on 16th September 1865, the fifth child of William Sale Sheavyn and his wife Jane Elizabeth (née Farmer). Her father was a draper and the family lived over the shop in Long Street opposite the Red Lion Hotel. Phoebe wrote an account of her life which she entitled "Personal Reminiscences of a Tradesman's daughter living in a small Country town, during the years 1870 - 1890" which, although not written until Phoebe was in her twenties, is a first-hand account of growing up in Victorian Atherstone. We are grateful to her great nephew, Brian Sheavyn for allowing us to use this record. She writes,

Most of the houses in the central part of Long Street were shops, with the family and employees living above. They had very deep cellars, cool for storing food. Many of these houses had once had gardens behind, but in the course of time some of these had been quite surrounded by buildings, leaving only a (paved) yard, with perhaps a solitary pear or apple tree clinging to a wall. Our own original garden had been shortened by an extension of the shop, and had become a mere yard. At the further end of the yard was, in my childhood, a stable for the pony or horse, and a cavity, under the warehouse, for dung from the stable. There was also a malodorous place called the privy, which frightened me. Dung was carried away eventually to the real garden outside the town, which had taken the place of our original one. There was a right of way from our yard to a side street. Not all the shop houses had as much yard space as we had. Many besides ourselves had warehouses, which sometimes left only a tiny yard, and still more had made use of the space behind the shop or house to build small tenements in a row, leaving a narrow passage access. These 'back-yards' as they were called housed the poorest of the people; they had no conveniences except one common to all, and many of them faced, across the narrow passage, a blank wall belonging to the next property. The back-yards were hotbeds of disease. The fever was bred in them, and there were frequent epidemics. A doctor who came to live in the town was shocked to find such conditions, but his efforts to improve them, valiant as they were, were hopeless, and he left the town. Most of the private houses, however, though all facing the next street, had preserved their gardens behind.

She describes the hierarchy of the town with the Dugdales at the top followed by lawyers and surgeons right down to tradespeople, of whom the butcher was the lowliest.

The butcher carried out his slaughtering at the end of his yard. I remember only too vividly, a night when I was living temporarily in the house next door. No sleep possible, for a poor little calf was moaning the whole time, as it slowly bled to death to provide white veal.

She writes of the hard work done by the women after a pig was killed and the difficulty of keeping bedding and clothing clean when all laundry had to be done in an outhouse where the copper had to be filled by buckets, then a fire lit under it to obtain hot water.

Occupations for men living in the backyards and small houses were limited. A few handymen were employed by the professional classes, and by many of the shopkeepers. A few were partially employed as gardeners. Some were needed to care for the horse and the pig, where these were kept. There was, of course, also butchering work to be done. Men not employed in the town worked in the collieries, a few miles away.

Later, a small factory for making hats was opened; but I do not know whether it employed men or women, or both.

The men spent their evenings mostly in the public houses, of which there were many; seven in the five minutes walk between our house and the station. So far as I know there were no rules as to hours of opening and closing.

For the daughters of working men, the one opening was domestic service. Every family, professional or trading, required them; but the need was hardly equal to the supply. Once engaged as domestic in a household, few dared to leave, whatever the conditions, lest no other job should turn up. Moreover, country girls were preferred. In our household we had a nurse and a kitchen maid, both from the country nearby.

The daughters of tradesmen generally became assistants in shops - their own father's or some shop in a near town, but those who wished to have more experience, or to learn a trade, went further afield. One of my sisters went to learn dressmaking in a large town; two went away to gain more experience as shop assistants. The fourth sister was blind, as a result of measles when one year old. For the more ambitious girls socially, there was a demand for family governesses, and it was also possible to start a school for small children. One or two girls of about my age became governesses, and one at least of them, a girl of character, became a trusted and influential person in the employer's household.

In the shops, (especially drapers' shops), in the larger towns, the system of "living in" prevailed. My eldest sister was sent away to learn dress-making, and, of course, "lived in". I remember being with my mother when she went by train to interview the head of the establishment after receiving some complaints from my sister. I was witness of a violent scene, which ended in my sister coming

away with us. She had been systematically starved until she could no longer bear it. She never recovered from the effects of this treatment, and died when twenty-one from what was then called "consumption of the bowels". A young half-brother also suffered from malnutrition as a result of "living in". He contracted tuberculosis of the lungs, and though he was removed, and sent to live in the country, when it was realised what was happening, he also never completely recovered, and died aged twenty-six. Two cases of death from malnutrition in one family.

Phoebe Sheavyn went on to become an academic, pioneering education for girls. She never married and her work took her to Oxford, Aberystwyth, London and the USA. Her final, and most influential post, was at Manchester University where she was warden of the first hall of residence for women students and where a building is named after her. However, she maintained her Atherstone roots coming home to her brother's house in Long Street to appear on all the censuses currently available.

Portrait of Phoebe Sheavyn in Sheavyn Hall, University of Manchester

A journal written by a young printer, J N Roper, apprenticed in Atherstone and 'living in' with his master, gives a boy's view of life in the town. He called it "Journal of some Pleasant and Comfortable Times at Atherstone, Warwickshire. Summer 1848". On April 12th he worked all night on a job for a Mr. Baker, keeping awake by drinking very strong coffee and eating about every two hours. Being allowed the next day off he went with a fellow apprentice by foot to Hartshill then to Witherley to deliver a book spending both lunchtime and evening smoking and drinking in two different pubs. This and hoping to see girls seems typical of his leisure time activities.

People would rise very early at 3.30-4.00 am to make the most of the daylight. Before starting work, some Atherstone menfolk would take a walk up to the Outwoods to have a game of cricket before work and, on occasion, enjoy a bottle of ginger beer. Whilst at the canal they would bathe or swim in it, however taking care not to cut their feet on pieces of flint. Early morning cricket followed by a swim is mentioned several times and must have been a regular occurrence.

Work for some would start at 8am. As there was no central heating, a fire would have to be lit before they started work. The large houses would have servants, some of whom started work aged 14. As there was no hot running water in these times, water would have to be heated in a copper to provide baths or for washing clothes. In the yards, several houses would have to share a copper in the washhouse and this could cause conflict as to who had the "best" washing day, which was generally a Monday.

Communication was by letter and people would write to their family, friends and sweethearts. Susanah, his young lady, included a lock of her hair neatly braided for the young apprentice on April 14th. She wrote again "in the usual strain" on the 22nd though there is no mention of young Mr. Roper writing to her anywhere near as often! His main correspondent seems to have been Nat Mawley, a friend from his home town of Gravesend. The two were intending to emigrate together to New South Wales in Australia despite parental opposition. As people had to move away from their family to find training opportunities, a letter from home with a local newspaper enclosed would have been most welcome. A local letter could be sent in the morning and a reply received in the evening. Letters to distant locations would be collected from local pubs and despatched from there.

Unlike Phoebe Sheavyn's step-brother, these apprentices seem to have been well fed, even on one occasion when the 'Governor' was out had "eaten and drank all that was on the table and made the servants cook some more" but they were criticised for reading in bed wasting the Governor's candles! They also seemed to be required at all times of day and night to take proofs or finished pamphlets around the town. Other duties such as pig killing also seemed to come into their terms of employment.

When smitten with a young girl, Kitty Hargrave, the young printer gathered flowers which he sent as a nosegay with a piece of poetry wrapped around it. It seems to have worked because the journal details several long moonlit walks which were "completely successful" whatever that might mean. On May 21st he wrote a farewell letter to Susanah and on the 24th he arranged to have the banns read at Mancetter church for his marriage to Kitty.

The Outwoods provided somewhere for Atherstone people to walk, rest and play. People would sit up on the hills to read letters and books and play games such as cricket and duck stone.

Evenings would be spent writing and reading by candlelight, maybe enjoyed with a pipe or a glass of ale, then a stroll before retiring to bed ready for the morning's early rise.

Sundays were a day to be spent at chapel in the morning to listen to the Sunday School sermon and hear the children in the choir sing. Before evening sermon, a pleasant time could be had by walking to several local places, the Outwoods always being popular, but also a walk to Witherley, Sheepy, Hartshill or Oldbury Reservoir, which, with a delightful companion, in the words of J N Roper, "seemed like paradise itself".

Records of Atherstone Parish Council 1894 to 1904

Parish Councils were brought about by the Local Government Act of 1894 and Atherstone is lucky to have a file of carbon copies of all letters written by the clerk in the first ten years of Atherstone Parish Council. The clerk was a Mr. William Alfred Hutton throughout this time. The letters reflect the times in being very formal always closing with

> "I have the honour to be
> my lords and gentlemen (or the addressee)
> your obedient servant

However, despite this difference in tone, the contents give an interesting insight into the matters of concern at that time which seem to have been very similar to those faced today ie. traffic – the level crossing at the station was causing delays and there were constant requests for its removal

> lack of land for building and a desire to expand the town boundaries
> repairs to roads and footpaths
> street lamps being broken by local youths
> bad behaviour, particularly in the Reading Room
> commercial traffic causing damage to property and street lamps
> lamps not being lit

The whole document makes interesting reading but some entries have direct relevance to Atherstone yards and their residents.

Lack of water was a problem at this time, with the Parish Council calling for a better supply on March 15th 1895 and again on June 6th 1898, when it was pointed out that cutting off the water supply to save stocks was a danger to the health and welfare of the inhabitants of Atherstone.

Bad behaviour was often attributed to boys resident in the yards such as the warning given to Samuel Barnsley of Collins Yard to control his son with regard to setting off the Fire Bell as a prank (April 2nd 1903) and the banning of Michael Grady from the Reading Room for disorderly conduct on February 10th 1904.

The running of the Reading Room was one of the duties of the Parish Council and as well as keeping order (three banning orders issued) they engaged a new Caretaker on October 1st 1895 and accepted donations of magazines to be available in the reading room in December 1902. Daily newspapers were kept there and were probably the only chance impoverished residents had of keeping up with the news.

The reading room was situated in the Coffee Tavern at the junction of Church Street and Long Street, which also served as a meeting place for many of the town's groups, including the Baddesley Pit Disaster Fund and the free soup distribution centre.

The Coffee Tavern on the corner of Long Street and Church Street

Two letters in the Council file point to the councillors wishing to provide a purpose-built library and, indeed, a letter dated March 10th 1904 to Andrew Carnegie refers to the offer of £1250 to erect a Free Public Library building in Atherstone but there is no indication that the offer was ever taken up.

The Parish Council seems to have administered some of the town's charities, particularly ones involving apprenticeships, which may have benefitted yard inhabitants, but more often letters by the clerk pointed to the problems caused by the yards. The yards were private land so not open to Police patrols, nor did they need to be lit by street lamps. Their narrowness and lack of adequate sanitation for the numbers living in them was a constant cause of concern. This letter written by the clerk really gives a clear picture of life in Atherstone's yards.

> *"Gentlemen.*
>
> *I am directed by the Atherstone Parish Council to request your attention to the following nuisance. On Monday last a very offensive Ash pit in Bingham's Yard was emptied and the contents were placed upon the Public Highway in Station Street. It is alleged that no disinfectants were used either at the time the excrement was in course of removal or afterwards and there is abundant evidence to prove that a most frightful stench existed in and about the locality for some days afterwards. Upon the occasion too the Contractor used a defective vehicle for the removal of the night soil and contents leaked from the wagon so that for a considerable distance not only in Station Street but also along the Watling Street Road night soil of a most offensive character was spilled upon the highway and allowed to remain there without being deodorised. The Parish Council trust the Rural District Council will see that Bye-laws No. 9, 10 and 11 are strictly enforced within the Township of Atherstone as these Bye-laws are amply sufficient to prevent the recurrence of such an intolerable nuisance as that which the Parish Council now desire to bring to your notice.*
>
> *Your obedient servant,"*

```
1898

Feb 19  Fielders Arms yard          wet  4 loads
  "  19  Corningley yard            dry  3   "
  "  19  Hinks    "    South st      "   4   "
  "  19  Adams  Long st              "   2   "
  "  21  Black horse yard           wet  3   "
  "  21  Hallam yard                dry  3   "
  "  21  Copson  Welcome st          "   1   "
  "  21  Beaconsfield Terrace        "   4   "
  "  21  Barrows Building Arden st    "   2   "
     24  Timbridge & Mason Long st    "   3   "
     25  Simonds Building Long st    wet  3   "
     25  Morgans Station st          dry  3   "
     25  Angle yard                   "   3   "
     26  Hayles  Owen st              "   4   "
     26  Brown Bear yard Long st      "   2   "
     26  Thurlow        "    st       "   1   "
     26  J Hitchen  North st   picked up "  2  "     up to here 1372 loads
  March 5th  Atherley Innage Terrace  "   3   "
     " 5  Wilson  Richmonds Road 2 holes dry 6  "
     " 5  Black Boy yard             Dry  2   "
     " 5  Taylors yard                "   3   "
```

The Contractor in this case was probably James Smith, a farmer, and we are indebted to another retired farmer, Mr. Trivett, for the loan of Mr. Smith's ledger for the years 1898 to 1914.

James Smith of Witherley Fields Farm and 2 South Street, Atherstone did many things to make a living. He was a landlord who owned properties around Atherstone, he also acted as a courier with his horses and carts. He bred cattle, sheep and pigs and kept a notebook of payments for the years from January 1898 to 1914.

The first pages are a record of his contract for removing 'soil' from the outside privies and ash pits around Atherstone on contract to Warwickshire County Council. All the yards were serviced as well as schools, the Police Station, shops and the homes of some of Atherstone's most illustrious residents. Waste was classified as wet or dry. The contents of privy buckets was classified as 'wet' and would be removed under cover of night. Many yard entries were too narrow to admit a cart so the open buckets would have to be carried the length of the yard.

Aspects of life in Victorian Atherstone that would have been known to residents of the yards

The Workhouse

A poorhouse was erected in Atherstone in 1723. It stood at the south end of Long Street which is now the site of the former Grammar School. It could accommodate up to sixty inmates with many more being assisted on 'out relief'. In the early 1800s, the inmates were employed in manufacturing cotton and in 1819, Henry Baker was employed to "undertake the management of the Cotton factory and Poor House." In 1834, a Royal Commission's report resulted in the Poor Law Amendment Act which was intended to put an end to all out-relief for the able bodied. The 15,000 or so parishes in England and Wales were formed into Poor Law Unions, each with its own union workhouse. A new workhouse was built to strict government specification on the opposite side of Long Street (Regal Court site) in 1835 and Atherstone Poor Law Union was formed on 31st March 1836. Its operation was overseen by an elected Board of Guardians, 18 in number, representing its 14 constituent parishes as listed below.

County of Warwick: Ansley, Atherstone, Baddesley Ensor, Baxterley, Bentley, Grendon, Mancetter, Merevale, Oldbury, Polesworth

County of Leicester: Atterton, Fenny Drayton, Sheepy Magna, Sheepy Parva.
Later Addition: Hartshill.

Long Street, Atherstone (from Hill Top). Workhouse on the left

In the 1881 census there were 69 residents in Atherstone's Union Workhouse. Many were elderly, including several married couples who would have been separated on entering the Workhouse. 8 inmates are listed as 'imbeciles' and a 30-year-old man is described as 'crippled from birth'. 2 women are in there with their families: Frances Ealing and her 5 children and Alice Pratt and her 3 children including William, aged 9 months. Conditions were intentionally hard with all able-bodied inmates expected to do work such as breaking rocks, sorting bones and unravelling rope so it could be re-used. The sexes were kept separately and children had very limited access to their parents.

Entertainment

The circus leaves the station along Long Street

In copies of local newspapers from the 1880s to the coming of television, there are numerous accounts of things to do in Atherstone. Over time the town has supported 3 cinemas and had halls where travelling plays and concerts were performed. The famous "Holloway's Travelling Theatre" came regularly to a pitch by the railway station and the circus used to visit the town.

There were hunt balls and dances in the Town Hall in what is now the Market Square, and picnics, galas and produce shows were held on the Outwoods and in the grounds of Merevale Hall.

A gala on the Outwoods

Atherstone had its own orchestra, bands and choirs, not to mention operatic and dramatic groups. Factories fielded football and cricket teams; they also took their workers on trips to the seaside as did the churches, pubs and clubs. Atherstone has always been famous for the number of its pubs. Much of the sport in town has been, and still is, organised through the network of pubs and clubs, as has entertainment. In the past the function rooms put on concerts and Bingo, now it is football on huge screens.

Atherstone has always enjoyed itself and there is nothing to say that the residents of the yards did not join in the leisure activities of the town in so far as they could afford to. Indeed, in looking through census records, the overall impression is that both men and women of working age seem to be employed. This may be because there was no welfare 'safety net' but it could also be that Atherstone was well supplied with work in shops, agriculture, the mines and hatting. Another factor noticed by our researchers is the way in which families looked after their own in Victorian times, with examples of how young women, widowed by war or accident, returned to the homes of their parents who then helped them raise their children. There are also examples of widows marrying the bachelor brothers or cousins of their late husband, thus securing a future for their children.

Education

For many children of poor parents the first education they received would be at church in the Sunday School. During the late 18th century, Sunday schools held at church or chapel became widely popular, receiving much charitable backing from the middle classes. They provided children from poor families with another opportunity to receive some basic learning, usually the ability to read.

The promoters of Sunday schools also became involved in the provision of regular day schools, and in 1811 the National Society for Promoting the Education of the Poor was formed to try to develop schooling in the growing industrial towns. The society was a Church of England body, and was able to make use of the parish organisation of the Society for Promoting Christian Knowledge (SPCK) and its 230 schools. One such school for boys was set up in Atherstone alongside the Grammar School in the Chancel of St. Mary's Church. Known as the English Free School, in 1842 it moved to new premises in South Street. An Infants' and Girls' School had been endowed in Ratcliffe Road, but prior to 1870 few of Atherstone's Yard children would have gone regularly to school.

The 1870 Education Act was the first piece of legislation to deal specifically with the provision of education in Britain. Most importantly, it demonstrated a commitment to provision on a national scale. The Act allowed voluntary schools to carry on unchanged, but established a system of 'school boards' to build and manage schools in areas where they were needed. The boards were locally elected bodies funded from the local rates and in 1878 Mr. Sale was elected Chairman of the Atherstone School Board and Joseph Bishop was appointed as the first School Attendance Officer.

However, this act did not address the problem of families preferring to send their children to work, rather than to school. The 1876 Royal Commission on the Factory Acts recommended that education be made compulsory in order to stop child labour. There is no evidence of child labour on a large scale in Atherstone, although it probably did exist in the factories and on farms. However, the age when children ceased to receive an allowance from the fund set up after the Baddesley Pit Disaster of 1882 was 13 years and one of the more poignant facts about that accident is that one of the miners whose body was never found was Joseph Scattergood, a miner working at the coal face aged only 15.

In 1880 a further Education Act finally made school attendance compulsory between the ages of five and ten, though by the early 1890s attendance was falling short at 82 per cent. Many children worked outside school hours - in 1901 the figure was put at 300,000 - and truancy was a major problem due to the fact that parents could not afford to give up income earned by their children. Fees were also payable until a change in the law in 1891. Further legislation in 1893 extended the age of compulsory attendance to 11, and in 1899 to 12. Despite schooling being made compulsory, school logs show that schools were often closed for long periods due to outbreaks of infectious diseases such as scarlet fever, diphtheria, smallpox and measles.

Compulsory education was also extended to blind and deaf children under the Elementary Education (Blind and Deaf Children) Act of 1893, which established special schools. Similar provision was made for physically-impaired children in the Elementary Education (Defective and Epileptic Children) Act of 1899.

In 1902 Parliament passed a new Education Act, drafted by AJ Balfour, which radically reorganised the administration of education at local level. It abolished the school boards in England and Wales. All elementary schools were placed in the hands of local education authorities, in the case of Atherstone, schools were administered by Warwickshire County Council.

The Act also, for the first time, made significant provision for secondary and technical education. Councils were encouraged, though not compelled, to subsidise existing grammar schools and to provide free places for working-class children. At last the sons of Atherstone's working families had a chance to 'sit' for entry to the Grammar School but girls had to travel to Nuneaton to gain anything more than an elementary education. For most schoolchildren education ended at the age of 12 years.

 The 1918 Fisher Act raised the school leaving age from 12 to 14 and made provision for a system of part-time 'continuation day' classes for those in work aged 14-18. It abolished all fees in state elementary schools and widened the provision of medical inspection, nursery schools, and special needs education. However, many of these innovative changes could only be implemented in part, or not at all, due to cuts in public expenditure forced by the economic depression of the 1920s. In Atherstone the old Boys' School closed and education settled into two red brick buildings, one South of Long Street and one North. Both schools catered for both boys and girls to leaving age with only the lucky few going to the Grammar School or to private schools. Atherstone Grammar School after nearly 400 years admitted girls in the 1920s. Around this time it also became clear that another school needed to be built to house the increasing population of the town and a senior school was built on the Cottagers' Piece on Witherley Road. Catholic children had their own school next to the Catholic Church in Owen Street.

By 1939 and the outbreak of war all the town's children were accommodated in local schools with a significant addition being the building of a Nursery School during the war to enable mothers to help with the war effort.

Mention has already been made of the Reading Room on the corner of Church Street which provided all of what we might now call 'Further Education'. Daily newspapers were available there and magazines donated by the better off. It also acted as a bookshop ordering academic books from London, which would arrive by train. In fact, the railway station would have played a much bigger part in the life of Atherstone residents than it does today. Seven Yards, now demolished, crowded in front of the railway building along with loco sheds, stables, cowsheds and a pigsty. In the station yard was the post and telegraph office and almost everything coming or leaving Atherstone came by rail, livestock, groceries, milk, vegetables, spare parts, hats, visitors and holidaymakers all passed through the station assisted by porters, many of whom lived in the yards. A delightful advertisement in a 1900 edition of the Atherstone News appealed for a porter to work at Atherstone Station "ability to milk would be an advantage".

Carriers with horse-drawn carts distributed goods to the town and outlying villages until they were replaced by lorries, vans and cars. Imagine the excitement in Atherstone the first time Canon Crawley-Boevey drove his family down to Atherstone station from the Vicarage at Grendon in this magnificent car.

Photograph courtesy of Elizabeth Crawley-Boevey, one of the little girls in the car

Health Services

As early as 1827 three local surgeons set up a dispensary in Atherstone to care for 'mechanics, servants, labourers' and their families for a small subscription. It opened for an hour 3 mornings a week but, unfortunately, it only functioned for 10 years due to financial difficulties depending , as it did, on donations from poor people and the good will of the doctors. On its closure Atherstone had no affordable medical care, the only facility being the new workhouse. Without money the residents of the yards had to rely on family, neighbours and charity for support. The Atherstone Blanket Loan Society was set up in 1871 and ran for 45 years lending out blankets for a small fee, but by far the most successful scheme was the Atherstone Nursing Association. Founded in 1892 and funded by subscriptions, donations and support from local businesses it paid the wages of a District Nurse who became a leading figure in the town. Her main problem was infection which spread like wildfire through the crowded yards. The smallpox outbreak of 1888 pointed up the lack of an isolation hospital for the district and a temporary tented hospital was set up between Mancetter and Hartshill. This was later replaced by temporary buildings which were still in use in 1911 despite it not having even a drinking water supply nor a laundry. Late in 1911 the new Isolation Hospital was opened at the foot of Archer's Hill on the Grendon side of Atherstone where infections could be isolated. Atherstone has never had a medical hospital, however, in 1900 the Manor Hospital was opened in Nuneaton built and run by public subscription from both Nuneaton and Atherstone. Prior to this and until it closed in 1932 the workhouse had provided the only hospital and geriatric service available to the poor of Atherstone.

It had been known for some time that disease could be spread by contact and in infected water but it was difficult to enforce a healthy lifestyle when children and adults shared toilets, bathing was difficult and many children slept four or five to a bed. Atherstone's prosperity had been partly founded on its dependable water supply from rivers and wells. In 1885 a new pumping house was opened at Birchley Heath providing piped water to the town. Unfortunately, demand exceeded supply and it was not until the 1920s that Atherstone had a full-time, clean water supply. Similarly an efficient sewage system was not achieved until a similar date, making it very difficult to improve the health of the Atherstone workforce.

Commemorative plaque on the Waterworks Pumping Station at Bentley

The First World War 1914 - 1918

It is not surprising that of the 171 Atherstone men killed in the war of 1914 -1918, nearly a quarter (38) came from the yards. All deaths are devastating to family and friends but to communities living in an enclosed yard the death of one young man must have affected all the families in that yard. Sadly some families lost more than one son. Mr. J Charnell of the Coach and Horses Yard lost two sons, Thomas, who was shot in the throat by a sniper at the end of October 1916, and Joseph, who was killed the following month. The Clamps, who lost three sons, Mr and Mrs W Ford of Cross Keys Yard ,who lost Edward, 19 and Henry, 26 , the Gisbornes of Allens Yard and the Richardsons of Old Plough Yard all suffered the loss of two of their boys, but one's heart goes out to Annie Llewellyn, a widow, who was the first mother to lose a son in the war. Arthur Llewellyn enlisted in the Coldstream Guards on June 4th 1914. He was shot through the head in Belgium on November 12th of the same year; he was aged 17. Another son, Albert Llewellyn, was a regular soldier who was taken prisoner in France and eventually died in January 1919.

We are indebted to the late Stafford Rees for this information.

Life in Atherstone pre and post-WWII from contemporary sources

The Atherstone Yards Project was largely brought about by a desire to record the memories of the few people remaining in Atherstone who could remember living in the yards. We have only been able to include a small number of those memories. One such memory was from Arthur Johnson, now in his 80s but with vivid memories of living first in Stephenson's Yard then in Roger's (or Rogerson's) Yard.

The house in Roger's Yard he remembers as being larger than the usual one-up-one-down in that it had a 'Parlour' used only at Christmas, with 2 bedrooms and an attic. He slept in the attic and from a tiny window he could see Hatton's hat factory and a piece of ground where the younger boys played football. The only source of heat and cooking was a coal-fired stove with an oven to one side which served as toaster, iron heater and hob. In winter his mother would wrap a blanket round the oven shelf for him to take up to bed with him. Later he had a stone hot water bottle. His father was a delivery man taking seed and supplies to farms, and he often came home with a chicken, goose or rabbit which his mother plucked and 'drew' (took out the insides) in the wash house. The main way of cooking was stewing but his mother was famous for making faggots out of cheaper cuts of meat put through the mincer.

Nothing was wasted. Just before they were demolished many of the houses had electric light but no one had a fridge as there was not enough room. Meat was kept in a 'meat safe' in the pantry which really only kept the flies off. The family never had bought fruit and sweets were rationed but the lads went scrumping for apples and pears in the autumn. There was an orchard called the 'Croft' where Croft Road now is and it had a wall all round it with glass set in concrete on top to keep the boys out, but they would work on a short section to remove the glass so they could climb over in the apple season!

Most of the entertainment was centred on the pubs or on sport. Atherstone Golf Club has produced four international golfers and several footballers started life in Atherstone. Pubs, factories and churches ran football and cricket teams and many of the games were played on the 'Level' on the Outwoods. In the pubs darts and dominoes were played all the time and good darts players were poached for the coming season like Premier League football players. Billiards was another obsession with some young men and the billiard hall at the junction of South Street and Coleshill Road had 14 tables, all busy at weekends. Although betting was illegal most games had an element of gambling. There were no betting shops but certain men were known to be Bookies' Runners who placed bets and handed out the winnings. On the Level younger boys would be placed as look-outs to spot policemen hoping to catch illegal gambling.

The Ball Game was a big event usually dominated by the mining families from Baddesley and Atherstone. The area of play was not limited like today and the younger men would like to get the ball in the canal knowing the older ones would give up if it meant many minutes in the freezing water. One year the son of Evans the coach company owner took the ball and ran right round Merevale Estate wall. He was a trained athlete and nobody could keep up with him; in other years the ball was spirited away by car.

More than once Mr. Johnson commented that in the 50s and 60s, when the yards were being cleared, the town was dominated by miners and the pubs were full of them. They worked days 6 – 2, afternoons 2 – 10 and nights 10 – 6 so there were always thirsty miners coming off shift.

Atherstone had two cinemas, the Regal and the Picturedrome, and you had to queue to see the good films. The only swimming pool was in the Grammar School yard and it was outdoors and unheated. Although much of his leisure time was spent in pubs, this was not the place to meet girls. Girls would go to the clubs in Grendon and Dordon but not into the pubs, and it was there that he met his wife. The Picturedrome in the old Corn Exchange building also served as a theatre for amateur plays and music and was a bit rougher than the more modern Regal. Another building known to the people who lived in the yards was the 'dole office' in the Albert Hall. Post Second World War work was easy to come by and, as Arthur Johnson remembers, "jobs were for life" enabling his mother to work part-time at the cinema, the school kitchen and in various cleaning jobs right up until retirement age.

As has already been said, mining dominated the town, and a regular sight and activity was the shovelling of the coal, paid as part of miners' wages, into the coal-hole or coalhouse. Arthur also remembers the war years when pigs were allowed to be kept in the yards to add to the food ration. People of his generation (born around 1930) witnessed the mass clearing of the yards and the dispersal of the tenants to various council estates in Atherstone and Mancetter. In the 1980s he, like many others, was able to buy his council house and pay off his mortgage before retiring. As he says

"You more or less looked after yourselves, you took the rent about 10 shilling a week I think…..
Our Landlord was named Tunbridge and he kept a butchers in Atherstone ……. I'd have been
a fool not to buy. I pay nothing now"

Raymond Barnes was born in the Coach and Horses pub but his parents moved to the Bluebell when he was about 18 months old. Raymond and his brother played in the Bluebell Yard, particularly in the three stables and the large room above them. Their 'toys' were grocery boxes from the Maypole store next door and whatever else they could find to play with as most of his memories were from the war years of 1939 to 45. By then the houses in the yards had been demolished so he and his brother were able to roam in the area that is now the bus station. Next door was Masters Bakery, where he fell through a window and came out covered in flour! There was also a hat factory where he, his brother and friends would climb over the gate and play diving into the bales of wool. Later the council built a shelter and a huge static water tank on the land behind the Bluebell and the boys built rafts to sail on the water intended for firefighting.

The big excitement of living in the Bluebell Inn was that it hosted the annual Atherstone Ball Game and the specially made giant ball was thrown out from Raymond's bedroom which overlooked Long Street. When Mr Barnes came out of the forces the family moved to a pub in Nuneaton but Raymond has fond memories of his boyhood spent in the yards of Atherstone.

The Blue Bell Inn on Ball Game day

Alphabetical List of Atherstone's Yards

Although there were at least 96 areas in Atherstone town centre known as yards, research has revealed many more names of yards as recorded in Government Census records (Appendix C), Clearance Orders (Appendix B) and Electoral Rolls. An assessment taken in 1768 indicates that there were many yards behind the houses and in the descriptions of the yards mention has been made that the yard may have existed from the era of 1768. A complete list follows this introduction.

Yards were often named for the public house that fronted Long Street, such as the Druids Arms Yard. Others took the name of the owner, so we have Wildays Yard and Fox Yard. Yards and the houses in them were often investment properties that were bought and sold, so the name might change as ownership changed. Cordingleys Yard, for example, was variously known as Collins Yard, Pearmans Yard, Whites Yard and Woodroffes Row, so a decision had to be made as to which named yard was to be described in further detail.

The 1911 Census is the last census publicly available, it was also the year that Dr Herring, Medical Officer of Health to the Atherstone Rural District Council, produced a damning report on the living conditions in Atherstone's yards and recommended wholesale demolition.(Appendix A) Therefore, these named yards are generally identified by the name by which they were known in 1911. However, some yards had ceased to exist by 1911 despite being lived in for 100 years or more, so these yards are listed by the final, or only, name by which they were known. Census records from 1841 to 1911, which form the basis of this research, were hand written so the spelling of names is 'flexible' and apostrophes have been left out.

To find a yard, first consult the complete list of yards in alphabetical order. This will tell you if it is a named yard and has its own entry, or it will say "See XXXX Yard". Every entry in the complete list tells you which map that yard is on, the yard number as designated by the Friends of Atherstone Heritage, and an indication of the street from which the yard was accessed and, in the case of Long Street, the probable house numbers between which the entrances to the yards were situated. To further aid identification a small photograph is included of what is physically there today (2012). This information has been gleaned from old maps and is as accurate as we can make it. Similarly, the information contained in each entry is accurate, but not complete. Researchers have tried to bring the yards to life, wherever possible, and all available photographs have been included.

One yard not included in the alphabetical list is **GAS HOUSE YARD**. This yard was off Coleshill Road beside the canal and was the site of Atherstone's gas works

Gas House Yard appears only once in 1861. Containing just 1 house with 2 occupants, a Mr William Lycett (56) is listed as working as a gas house fitter, his wife Betsy is listed as "ditto wife". In the area round the gas works there were houses for the manager and engineer so it was not a true yard. It is interesting to note that, although gas street lights were installed in Long Street as early as 1850, there were never any street lights in the yards because they were private property. For the same reason the Police did not routinely patrol the yards, unless responding to a crime.

Alphabetical list of yard names

Yard Name	Map Number	Yard No	Long Street No.	
Allens Yard	8	100	141-143	
Angel Yard	2	26	Church St	
Ashers Yard	9	123	83-85	See Woods Yard (124)
Avins Yard	10	158	23-25	
Baker Terrace	10	152	Station St	Also known as Simonds Yard (153) Nurthalls Yard (154)
Bakers Yard	4	42	136-138	Also known as Millers Yard (41) Bakers Yard (42) Veros Yard (43) Taylors Yard (44)
Barnes Yard	9	132	67-69	See Spencers Yard (133)
Barsbys Yard	5	76	202-204	See Mercers Buildings (74)
Bassetts Yard	8	109	109-111	See Stevensons Yard (112)
Baxters Buildings/ Knob Hill	7	84	South St	
Biddles Yard	7	91	167-169	See Sales Yard (92)
Binghams Row	10	142	37-39	See Willdays Yard (141)
Black Boy Yard	9	120	91-93	
Black Horse Yard	4	51	156-158	
Blowers Yard	2	21	62-64	Also known as Hollybush Yard (20)
Blue Bell Yard	9	121	87-89	
Bonds Yard	8	98	141-143	Also known as Briggs Yard (99)
Boss Yard	10	159	19-21	
Bournes Yard	8	102	131-133	
Briggs Yard	8	99	141-143	See Bonds Yard (98)
Brooks Yard	4	36	124-126	Also known as Hoggs Yard (35) and Westons Yard (34)
Brown Bear Yard	2	19	46-48	Also known as Jeffcotts Yard (18)
Clarks Yard	11	118	Station St	
Cleoburys Yard	1	6	16-18	Also known as Windridges Yard (7)
Coach & Horses Yard	8	101	135-137	
Coles Yard	4	56	164-166	See Cotton Mill Yard (55)
Collins Yard	10	144	33-35	See Cordingleys Yard (143)
Congreves Yard	5	62	176-178	Also known as Kendricks Yard (58) Silks Court (59) Windridges Yard (60) Quimby Yard (61)
Co-op Yard	9	137	59-61	

Copes Yard/ Buildings	5	68	196-198	See Pittams Yard (67)
Corbetts Yard	7	86	167-169	See Simonds Yard (89)
Cordingleys Yard	10	143	33-35	Also known as Collins Yard (144) Pearmans Yard (145) Whites Yard (146) Woodroffes Row (147)
Cotton Mill Yard	4	55	164-166	Also known as Coles Yard (56)
Cross Keys Yard	4	49	146-148	Also known as Rowleys Yard (48)
Crown Yard	1	17	44-46	
Dolphin Yard	4	54	162-164	
Druids Arms Yard	9	129	67-69	Also known as Marriotts Yard (130)
Earps Yard	10	156	17-19 Dem	See Johnsons Buildings (155)
Ellis Yard	4	38	134-136	See Old Plough Yard (40)
Everetts Yard	8	107	109-111	See Radford Buildings (108)
Factory Yard	9	136	63-65	Also known as Handford Yard (135)
Farmers Yard	5	72	202-204	See Mercers Buildings (74)
Fords Yard/ Buildings	2	22	64-66	Also known as Wimburys Buildings (23)
Fox Yard	11	115	Coleshill Rd	
Friars Yard	1	13	30-32	See White Bear Yard (12)
Friends Meeting House	5	57	172-174	
Gains Yard	7	95	149-151	See Kitchins Yard (96)
Garden Row	1	5	14-16	
Gees Yard	8	105	113-115	See Hattons Yard (106)
Gisbournes Yard	7	82	179-181	Also known as Potters Yard (81) Lucas Yard (83)
Gothards Row/Yard	5	63	178-180	See Mount Pleasant Yard (64)
Gutteridge Yard	9	122	83-85	See Woods Yard (124)
Haddons Yard	7	88	167-169	See Simonds Yard (89)
Haddons Yard	11	116	Station St	
Hallams Yard/Sq	7	85	171-173	
Hambreys Yard	8	111	109-111	See Stevensons Yard (112)
Hand & Bottle Yard	9	125	81-83	
Handford Yard	9	135	63-65	See Factoty Yard (136)
Hat and Beaver Yard	4	37	128-130	
Hattons Yard	4	46	142-144	See Hudsons Yard (47)
Hattons Yard	8	106	113-115	Also known as Gees Yard (105)
Heatles Buildings	7	80	181-183	Also known as Whites Yard (79)

Hincks Yard	8	104	123-125	
Hoggs Yard	4	35	124-126	See Brooks Yard (36)
Hollybush Yard	2	20	62-64	See Blowers Yard (21)
Hudsons Yard	4	47	142-144	Also known as Hattons Yard (46)
Hulls Yard	7	87	167-169	See Simonds Yard (89)
Innage Terrace	11	119	Station St	
Jeffcotts Yard	2	18	46-48	See Brown Bear Yard (19)
Johnsons Buildings	10	155	17-19 Dem	Also known as Earps Yard (156)
Kendricks Yard	5	58	176-178	See Congreves Yard (62)
Kent Yard	7	93	163-165	See Radford Buildings (108)
Kings Arms Yard	9	127	73-75	
Kitchens Yard / Buildings	7	96	149-151	Also known as Gains Yard (95)
Lagoes Court/ Buildings	1	9	20-26	
Lawtons Yard	4	45	136-138	See Bakers Yard (42)
Lloyds Yard	9	134	67-69	See Spencers Yard (133)
Lucas Yard	7	83	179-181	See Gisbournes Yard (82)
Marriotts Yard	9	130	67-69	See Druids Arms Yard (129)
Mays Yard	4	50	150-152	
Meads Yard	1	3	8-10	Also known as Ortons Yard (2)
Mercers Buildings	5	74	202-204	Also known as Farmers Yard (72) Paynes Yard (73) Barsbys Yard (76)
Millers Yard	3	29	94-96	
Millers Yard	4	41	136-138	See Bakers Yard (42)
Millers Yard	5	71	200-202	See Pearmans Yard (70)
Mills Yard	5	65	186-188	
Mount Pleasant	5	64	178-180	Also known as Gothards Row (63)
Mousleys Yard	7	90	167-169	See Sales Yard (92)
Mustons Yard	1	15	34-36	See Rogers Buildings (16)
Mustons Yard	3	30	100-102	See Pinchbacks Yard (31)
Nelson Yard	9	126	75-77	
Nurthalls Yard	10	154	Station St	See Bakers Terrace (152)
Old House Yard	8	103		
Old House Yard 2	10	160	13-15 Dem	
Old Plough Yard	4	40	134-136	Also known as Wrights Yard (39) Ellis Yard (38)
Ormes Yard	2	27	Church St	
Ortons Court/Yard	1	2	8-10	See Meads Yard (3)
Ortons Yard	5	66	196-198	See Pittams Yard (67)

Partridges Yard	9	131	67-69	See Spencers Yard (133)
Paynes Buildings	5	73	202-204	See Mercers Buildings (74)
Paynes Lodging House	6	78	189-191	
Paynes Yard	4	53	160-162	Also known as Smiths Yard (52)
Pearmans Yard	5	70	200-202	Also known as Vinraces Yard (69) Millers Yard (71)
Pearmans Yard	10	145	33-35	See Cordingleys Yard (143)
Phoenix Yard	2	24	Church St	Also known as Simmonds Yard (25)
Pinchbacks Yard	3	31	100-102	Also known as Mustons Yard (30)
Pittams Yard	5	67	196-198	Also known as Ortons Yard (66) Copes Buildings (68)
Potters Yard	7	81	179-181	See Gisbournes Yard (82)
Quimbys Yard	5	61	176-178	See Congreves Yard (62)
Radford Yard	8	108	109-111	Also known as Everetts Yard (107)
Radfords Buildings/ Yard	7	94	163-165	Also knoan as Kent Yard(93)
Railway Tavern Yard	10	163	Demolished	
Ram Yard	1	10	28-30	Also known as Whites Yard (11)
Richmond Hill Yard	11	114	Coleshill Rd	
Road Knights Yard	10	151	25-27	See Veros Yard (150)
Roes Yard	1	14	34-36	See Rogers Buildings (16)
Roes Yard	10	140	Station St	
Rogers Buildings/ Yards	1	16	34-36	Also known as Roes Yard (14) Mustons Yard (15)
Rogers Yard	9	138	49-51	See Swan and Two Necks Yard (139)
Rowleys Yard	4	48	146-148	See Cross Keys Yard (49)
Rumseys Yard	1	4	10-12	
Sales Yard / Buildings	7	92	167-169	Also known as Mousleys Yard (90) Biddles Yard (91)
Sands Yard	8	110	109-111	See Stevensons Yard (112)
Silks Court	5	59	176-178	See Congreves Yard (62)
Simmonds Yard	2	25	Church St	See Phoenix Yard (24)
Simonds Yard	10	153	Station St	See Bakers Terrace (152)
Simonds Yard / Buildings	7	89	167-169	Also known as Corbetts Yard (86) Hulls Yard (87) Haddons Yard (88)
Smiths Yard	4	52	160-162	See Paynes Yard (53)
Spencers Yard	10	157	17-19 Dem	See Johnsons Buildings (155)
Spencers Yard/ Buildings	9	133	67-69	Also known as Partridges Yard (131) Barnes Yard (132) Lloyds Yard (134)

Stantons Buildings	5	75	202-204	
Stevensons Yard	8	112	109-111	Also known as Bassetts Yard (109) Sands Yard (110) Hambreys Yard (111)
Swan and Two Necks Yard	9	139	49-51	Also known as Rogers Yard (138)
Swan Yard	3	28	North St	
T Veros Yard	9	128		
Tates Yard	10	162	Station St Dem	
Taylors Yard	4	44	136-138	See Bakers Yard (42)
Throwers Yard	1	8	20-22	
Veros Yard	4	43	136-138	See Bakers Yard (42)
Veros Yard	10	161	9-11 Dem	
Veros Yard/Terrace	10	150	25-27	Also known as Roadknights Yard (151)
Vinraces Row	3	32	118-120	
Vinraces Yard	5	69	200-202	See Pearmans Yard (70)
Wash Pad Yard	10	164	Station St Dem	
Westons Yard	4	34	124-126	See Brooks Yard (36)
Wheatsheaf Yard	10	149	29-31	
Whitbys Yard	3	33	122-124	
White Bear Yard	1	12	30-32	Also known as Friars Yard (13)
White Hart Yard	1	1	White Hart	
White Lion Yard	11	117	Station St	
Whites Court	1	11	28-30	See Ram Yard (10)
Whites Yard	7	79	181-183	See Heatles Yard (80)
Whites Yard	10	146	33-35	See Cordingleys Yard (143)
Wildays Yard	10	141	37-39	Also known as Binghams Yard (142)
Wimburys Buildings	2	23	64-66	See Fords Yard (22)
Windridges Yard	1	7	16-18	See Cleoburys Yard (6)
Windridges Yard	5	60	176-178	See Congreves Yard (62)
Winters Yard/ Terrace	8	113	103-105	
Woodman Yard	10	148	Station St	
Woodruffes Row	10	147	33-35	See Cordingleys Yard (143)
Woods Yard	9	124	83-85	Also known as Gutteridges Yard (122) Ashers Yard (123)
Woolpack Yard	8	97	145-147	
Wrights Yard	4	39	134-136	See Old Plough Yard (40)
Wrights Yard	5	77	204-206	

Map Ref: 8	Yard No. 100	Long Street 141-143

First known in 1768 – 1 house.

The houses in this yard were compulsory purchased and demolished in 1957.

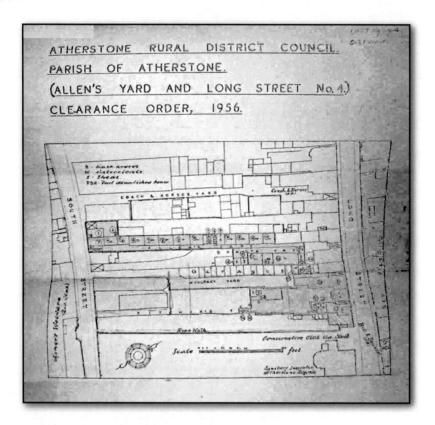

This yard had 13 houses with up to 58 people sharing a washhouse and 6 privies.

A clearance order dated July 1956 prepared by the Sanitary Inspector shows a scale map with properties in Allens Yard, Bonds Yard and numbers 147, 149 and 151 Long Street with outbuildings all due for demolition. Allens Yard was accessible from South Street and it is difficult to know if this was one yard with two names, or two different yards.

Newspaper article, Atherstone News, dated 25 September 1891.

"In company with the Medical Officer of Health, the Surveyor (Mr Chipperfield) had visited Allens Yard and, at the time of inspection, found the ashpit full and the hopper closets blocked. There were only three closets in the yard, one of which was kept locked, so only two closets were available for the use of over 58 persons. In the house next to the closets was a case of fever. The usual notices were ordered to be served."

Sylvia Maddox recalls the front room of their house being used as a TV repair shop run by Fred Hogg. Unusually the house had a large attic and a cellar.

ANGEL YARD

Map Ref: 2	Yard No. 26	Church Street

First known in 1768 – 1 house.

The houses in this yard were demolished in 1937.

The 1861 census noted one house uninhabited.

Occupations included coal miners, grocer's porter, butcher's apprentice, coachman, joiner, insurance agent.

Herring Report (1911) recorded 6 houses with 30 occupants (22 adults and 8 children).

These houses were described as having one room on the ground floor with a bedroom and a landing bedroom upstairs.

This yard had 6 houses with up to 30 people.

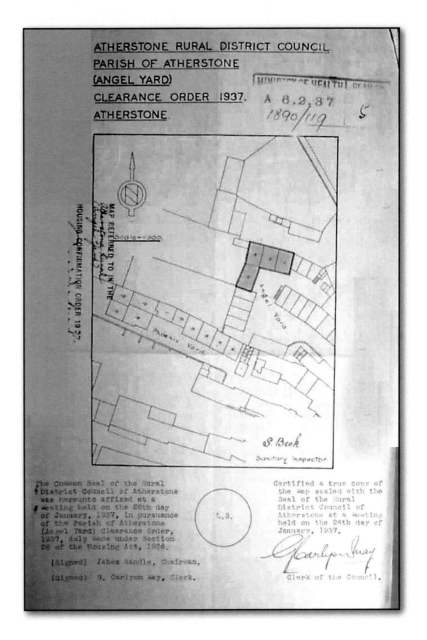

Map Ref: 10	Yard No. 158	Long Street. 23-25

First known in 1768 – 2 houses.

Not in 1851 Census.

The yard was demolished in 1936.

This yard had 23 houses with up to 83 people.

Although only officially recorded in the 1841 census part of Avins Yard was built in the eighteenth century. These were small back to back houses. In the 19th Century taller houses were built to accommodate the growing population. It appears to have merged with Nurthalls Yard. In 1841 there were 4 houses and 9 people. It was not recorded in 1861 but reappears in 1871 with 23 houses and 83 people.

In the 1951-1957 electoral roll records there was just one house inhabited by a Mr and Mrs Watts.

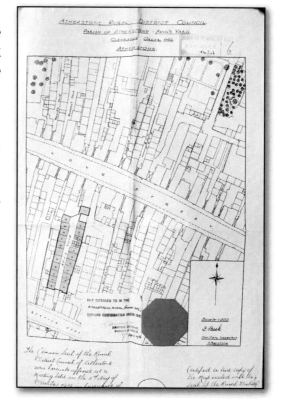

BAKER TERRACE

This yard had 7 houses with up to 30 people.

Map Ref: 10	Yard No. 152	Station Street

First known in 1881.

Also known as **NURTHALLS YARD** 1841 1861 **SIMONDS YARD** 1851.

This yard was part of the 1956 clearance.

Only appears in 1881 census. Again this yard has a large number working in the hatting trade.

BAKERS YARD

This yard had 3 houses.

Map Ref: 4	Yard No. 42	Street No. 136-138

First recorded in 1871 and recorded to 1911.

Also known as **LAWTONS YARD** in 1947.

May also have been known as **TAYLORS YARD, VEROS YARD** and **MILLERS YARD.**

There was a clearance order on 3 houses served for this yard in 1937 but the name appears on the Electoral Roll for 1947. In 1956, under the name of Bakers Yard, buildings were cleared from this area but they were mainly privies and sheds.

Although only a small yard the area seems to have been occupied continuously except for 1901 when it does not appear on the census.

BAXTERS BUILDINGS/COTTAGES

Map Ref: 7	Yard No. 84	South Street

First known in 1861.

Also known as **KNOB HILL** in 1881.

The houses in this yard were demolished in 1961.

We have a copy of a letter sent by the Ministry of Housing & Local Government, Whitehall, London, SW1 dated the 11th September 1961 confirming the Clearance Order but also, in accordance with Section 60 of the Housing Act 1957, directing the Council to make well-maintained payments in respect of nos. 3 and 4 Baxters Buildings. These were to compensate owners for habitable buildings which fell within a Clearance Area.

This yard had 5 houses with up to 20 people sharing 5 privies.

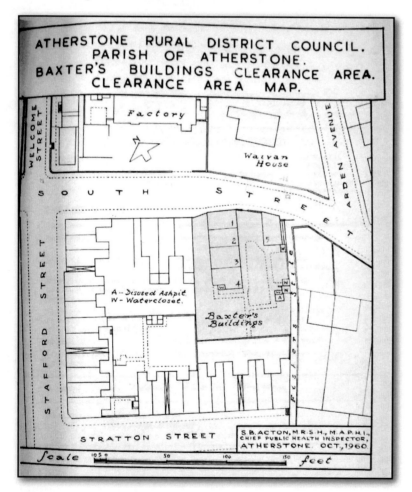

Baxters Buildings are likely to be named for the Baxter family who were a wealthy and influential family living in Atherstone from the 1650's. By 1800 they owned all the backland in South Street down to Owen Street and as far back as the Outwoods.

In 1786 they bought the Lordship of the Manor of Atherstone from the Repingtons and sold it to the Dugdales in 1811. Stafford Street. Stratton Street and Dudley Street are also named after the family.

BLACK BOY YARD

This yard had 1 house with only 2 people.

Map Ref: 9	Yard No. 120	Long Street 91-93

First known in 1768 – 1 house.

The first mention of the Black Boy Yard on census records is in 1851. The Yard only contained 1 house so must have seemed quite exclusive compared to some of the very large and overcrowded yards .

The Black Boy Inn fronted onto Long Street. Like most of the yards on the south side of Long Street, the Yard ran through to Station Street, coming out opposite the White Lion pub.

From between 1851 and 1871 a mother and daughter lived in the Yard. Hannah Bassett (64) a widow working as a charwoman, had a daughter Anne (35) who was deaf and dumb. In 1861 Hannah was working as an upholstress as is Anne. In 1871 Hannah is now alone still working, her daughter is no longer listed. In 1881 the Yard is no longer listed.

By 1891 the census shows a gentleman aged 65 living in the house, he is classed as an army pensioner. If we were to estimate he was born in 1826, he could possibly have served in the Crimean War of 1856. Unfortunately his surname is illegible from the census records so we cannot look him up any further.

In 1901 the house is unoccupied.

BLACK HORSE YARD

Map Ref: 4	Yard No. 51	Long Street 156-158

Built pre 1841 and lived in until 1934.

Condemned by the Herring Report of 1911 this yard was finally demolished in 1935 when eight of the houses belonged to a Mrs M E P Markham.

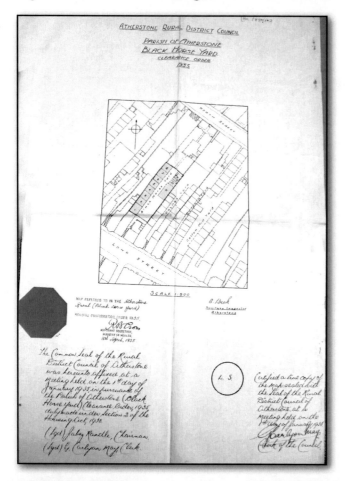

This yard had 9 houses with up to 41 people sharing 1 washhouse, a tap/pump and 4 privies.

BLOWERS YARD

Map Ref: 2	Yard No. 21	Long Street 62 - 64

Only recorded in 1901.

Also known as **HOLLYBUSH YARD 1891**.

1901 census – Occupied by a coal miner and his family.

This yard had 1 house with up to 4 people.

BLUE BELL YARD

Map Ref: 9	Yard No. 121	Long Street 87-89

First known in 1768 – 3 houses and inhabited continuously until 1924.

The houses in this yard were demolished in 1926.

The Blue Bell Yard houses were built behind the Blue Bell Inn. The Yard and pub have long gone, along no doubt with many happy memories of the home of the Atherstone Ball Game on Shrove Tuesday. The ball would be thrown from the upstairs window of the Blue Bell Inn, along with pennies and sweets.

This yard had up to 8 houses with up to 34 people.

Atherstone Centre, Long Street.

From an oral history given by Mr Raymond Barnes who lived in the Bluebell Inn between 1937 and 1946, we have his memories of the Yard. He recalls there being a well near to the scullery of the living quarters of the pub. Originally a coaching inn, the yard contained 3 stables with a large clubroom over. He recalls the entrance to the yard with Masters Bakery on the left hand side and the Bluebell to the right. His bedroom was at the front and he shared a double bed with his brother, his mother had another double bed whilst his father was away at war. He recalls the ball being thrown from his bedroom, which was at the front facing onto Long Street, the ball being made by a cobbler from Atherstone who only had one leg.

Between the Bluebell Yard and Master's part of the Yard, ran a low central wall separating the two properties.

Mr Barnes remembers the houses in the Yard were pulled down before the Second World War. The Council built an air raid shelter on the Station Street end of the Yard and "an enormous great circular water tank" on open ground at the top end of Bluebell Yard off Station Street.

BONDS YARD

Map Ref: 8	Yard No. 98	Long Street 141-143

First known in 1768 – 3 houses.

Also known as **BRIGGS YARD** 1861.

The houses in this yard were compulsory purchased and demolished in 1957.

This yard was divided by a low wall from Allen's Yard and was part of the Allen's Yard and Long Street No.4 Clearance Order 1956.

Newspaper article, Atherstone News, dated 25 September 1891.

In an Inspection by the Surveyor (Mr Chipperfield) accompanied by the Medical Officer: "There were two pigstys in which they saw several pigs, the stys not being more than six yards away from the nearest house, and were at that time in a dirty state." The usual notices were ordered to be served.

This yard had 2 houses with up to 13 people sharing a washhouse, a tap/pump and 2 privies.

BOSS YARD

| Map Ref: 10 | Yard No. 159 | Long Street 19-21 |

First known in 1768 – 3 homes.

Does not appear in 1911 census but is known as Boss Yard in 1937 on demolition order. This and Johnsons Yard may have had the same entrance to Long Street.

This yard had 5 houses with up to 24 people.

Tom Johnson who owned the 3 houses in Boss Yard states that the houses had been improved. He also stated that he did not accept families with children although there was a young couple with a baby in one house born after his appeal. The others were rented to elderly people. Johnson had to admit there was no direct water supply to the houses.

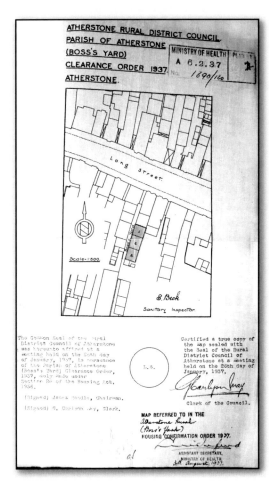

There were three cottages in the yard in 1937 each with 1 living room and 1 bedroom. These were back to back houses. These types of houses had been prohibited 60 years before. Tom Johnson acquired these houses in 1910. He was also a bookmaker and dealer from Leicester. He and his family lived at 21 Long Street. They had 9 children. The house had a living room 12 ft. x 11 ft. x 7 ft.6 in. bedroom 14 ft. x 11 ft. x 6 ft. to 7 ft.6 in. high.

In 1901 one house was occupied by William Cook, a general labourer aged 48, his 6 children, his married sister, his father and his nephew. Tom Johnson states in the enquiry that the washhouse could be used by the inhabitants 2 days a week. The water closet had no flushing. There was one tap in the yard for the use of the three houses.

BOURNES YARD

Map Ref: 8	Yard No. 102	Long Street 131-133

The census for 1891 and 1901 record this yard but not in the 1911 census, however, it reappears in the electoral rolls between 1924 and 1934. No confirmed date for demolition.

BROOKS YARD

Map Ref: 4	Yard No. 36	Long Street 124-126

Recorded sporadically but called Brooks Yard in 1911.

Also known as **WESTONS YARD** 1841 1851 and **HOGGS YARD** 1891.

Map Ref: 2	Yard No. 19	Long Street 46-48

First known in 1768 – 15 houses. In censuses from 1871 – 1911 with people still on the Electoral Register until 1956.

Also known as **JEFFCOTTS YARD** 1851 and 1861 census.

The houses in this yard were demolished in 1957 despite being condemned by Herring in 1911.

This yard had 15 houses with up to 21 people.

2 houses were owned by a Mr A V Green and each had a Gross Value of £10 and Rateable Value of £6. The 1871 census showed 3 inhabited and 2 uninhabited houses. Occupations have included: painter, hatters, dressmaker, bricklayers and labourer. The Herring Report listed 3 houses with 13 adults and children.

CLARKS YARD

Map Ref: 11	Yard No. 118	Station Street

Built pre 1841 and lived in continuously until 1969

Clarks Yard was located on Station Street, the entrance can still be seen.

Clarks Yard has been listed as containing between 7 and 9 houses, housing from between 14 people in 1841, to a maximum of 35 in 1881, however the average equates to around 27 occupants in the yard over the decades.

In 1901 the census stated there are now 9 houses, housing 29 adults and children.

From the 1881 and 1891 census, Thomas Clark is living in one of the houses, working as a butcher.

This yard had 9 houses with up to 35 people living in the Yard.

From an article in the Atherstone News dated 25th September 1891, there is mention of swine flu in the yard and mention of there possibly being 2 pig sties in the yard.

CLEOBURYS YARD

This yard had 4 houses with up to 13 people.

Map Ref: 1	Yard No. 6	Long Street 16-18

First known in 1768 and lived in continuously until 1960.

Also known as **WINDRIDGES YARD** 1891 - 1911.

Date of demolition 1965.

This Yard is condemned in The Herring Report 1911 as having 4 houses with 10 occupants – 8 adults and 2 children.

CO-OP YARD

Map Ref: 9	Yard No. 137	Long Street 59-61

Access from Station St.

This yard is only recorded once in the 1911 census.

This yard had 4 houses with up to 13 people.

Map Ref: 8	Yard No. 101	Long Street 135-137

First known in 1768 and occupied until 1954.

The houses in this yard were demolished in 1937. This was one of the yards behind public houses so, although the yard was demolished in 1937, the Coach and Horses pub remained in business until the 1970s when it was cleared to create Woolpack Way and a car park. Clearing of the yards revealed a 'bottle kiln' used by Sale's to store grain.

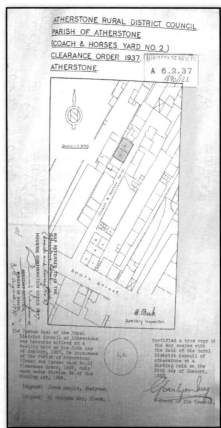

This yard had up to 21 houses with up to 108 people sharing 2 washhouses, a tap/ pump and 3 privies.

Map Ref: 5	Yard No. 62	Long Street 176-178

Built pre 1841. First known as Congraves in 1901

Also known as **KENDRICKS YARD** 1841-51 **SILKS COURT** 1861 **WINDRIDGES YARD** 1871-81 and **QUIMBYS YARD** 1891.

A Clearance Order for the demolition of this Yard dated 30 August 1937 lists 2 Dwelling Houses a washhouse, a watercloset and an ashpit. The owner is a Mr Charles Taylor.

This yard had up to 6 houses with up to 26 people. By 1901 there were 2 houses with 1 washhouse and a privy.

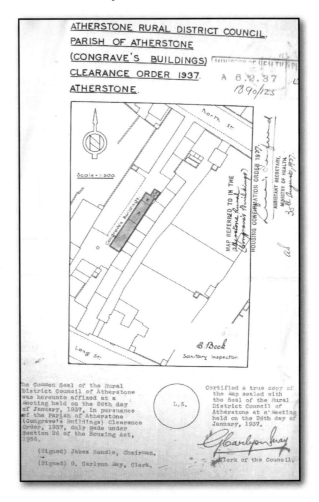

From the 1861 census we know that immediately before Silks Court was a lodging house with a Mr Joseph Windridge as its keeper. By the 1871 census Maria Windridge, widow of Joseph, has taken over and now has Windridge Lodging House Yard which continues through to the 1881 census where Maria is now 80 years old. In 1891 there is a lodging house immediately before Quimbys Yard.

Martha Congrave is a widow living on her own means at 176 Long Street on the 1901 Census and may have given her name to the Yard. Details of 'Values in respect of Yard Properties in Atherstone' from the early 1930's lists 2 properties belonging to Congrave & Taylor with a rateable value of £5 each.

CORDINGLEYS YARD

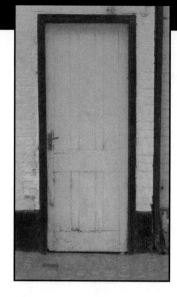

Map Ref: 10	Yard No. 143	Long Street 33-35

First known in 1911 but houses built in 1780's.

Also known as **WOODRUFFES ROW** 1841-61 **WHITES YARD** 1871 **PEARMANS YARD** 1881 and **COLLINS YARD** 1891.

The houses in this yard were demolished in 1935 with all 14 listed heads of household moving out on either the 16th 23rd or 30th September 1935 and moving to North Street. At the time they were paying between 5/6 and 7/- rent per week and this would increase for their new homes to between 6/9 for two beds and 8/7 for a four bedroomed house.

In a newspaper article in the Atherstone News dated 29 September 1933 Mr S Beck, the Sanitary Inspector, stated the difficulty in this Yard was not so much the number of occupants but the congestion of the houses.

Cordingleys and a second row of houses Willdays Terrace were virtually back to back with a twitchell and following inspection were in the first instalment of the councils five year plan for demolition.

This yard had 14 houses with up to 59 people sharing 3 washhouses and 9 privies.

In a letter to the Minister of Health dated 14 January 1935 Mr G F Collins objected against the order re stores, warehouse etc. in Cordingleys Buildings on the grounds 'that this property is at the rear and attached to shops nos. 33 and 35 Long Street and is used to carry on the business and therefore indispensable, and 'being business premises does not come under the act'.

A public enquiry was held on 12th February 1935. Mr Dixon representing the owners of numbers 3-19, Mrs Agnes Mary and Gertrude Alice Ellis, and numbers 20-25 on the order, Mr GF Collins, cross examined Dr Fisher and Mr Beck on their reports recommending demolition. The age of the houses at this time was given as over 150 years with Mr Dixon asserting that the houses were in 'a very good state of repair and compare very favourably with those on the main street'. A local builder, Mr Holland, had prepared a plan involving demolition of alternate pairs of houses, damp proofing, erecting new sculleries and pantries on the end of each remaining house and existing outbuildings repaired at a cost of approx. £60 per house. Mr Collins, the owner of properties in Willdays Terrace as well as Cordingleys, stated that 'the twitchel was properly drained' and there was 'ample room for a man to go up between my property and the other'. Both Dr Fisher and Mr Beck were of the opinion that even if work was done, the houses would still not comply with all regulations and would still be subject to demolition.

The Clearance Order was confirmed in March 1935 with some outbuildings, including a slaughterhouse used as a store, allowed to remain.

COTTON MILL YARD

Map Ref: 4	Yard No. 55	Long Street 164-166

First known in 1768 – 15 houses and running from Long Street to North Street.

Also known as **COLES YARD** 1851

Named for the Cotton Mill which was built to provide work for the inmates of the Poor House next door, the yard had between 18 and 22 houses with up to 9 houses sharing a washhouse with 2 coppers and 4 water closets.

Samuel Deeming, a Master Shoemaker/Cordwainer, and his family can be traced living in the Yard from1851-1891 with up to 8 living under the same roof with a living room and 2 bedrooms.

In 1937 following an Inspection of the yard 11 dwelling houses were found to be unfit for human habitation and a Clearance Order was issued. In response to this Mr Frank Coleman, the owner of the properties, instructed his solicitors to write to the Minister of Health proposing that the house, numbered 1 on the map, be added to 168 Long Street; that the water closets, washhouse and ashpit be retained for use by the tenants in adjoining houses and that numbers 16-17 be altered to be made fit for habitation. No objection was raised for the demolition of the houses numbered 2-9, although there are plans that show Mr Coleman was considering demolishing 4 and improving 4.

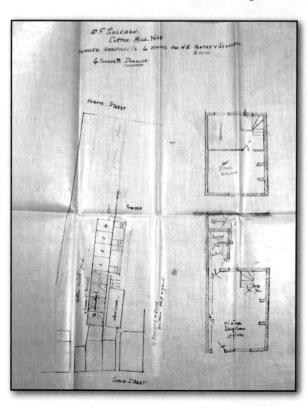

From a Sanitary Inspector's map of 1956 we can see that house 1 together with the outbuildings were retained from the original Clearance Order and that the remaining 8 houses, with steps leading down to the frontages, and all out buildings at the North Street end of the Yard were cited for demolition. All buildings were removed by 1958 with some families being rehoused in North Street.

CROSS KEYS YARD

Map Ref: 4	Yard No. 49	Long Street 146-148

First known in 1768 – 3 houses and inhabited continuously until 1936.

Also known as **ROWLEYS YARD** in 1841.

The houses in this yard were demolished in 1936, although singled out for demolition in the Herring Report of 1911.

Barry Ford, to whom we are indebted for photographs and information, came forward to tell us about his grandfather, Sam Ford. Little was known of him except that he came from 'the yards' but by searching the Internet we have been able to trace him literally from the cradle to the grave.

This yard had up to 15 houses with up to 54 people sharing 4 washhouses, a tap/ pump and 7 privies.

This photograph shows 'Sam' sitting in one of Atherstone's yards with two of his sons, William, Barry's father, is in front of him and Sid (uncle) on his left. Unfortunately, although we have found out a great deal about granddad Sam, we are not sure which yard he lived in when this photograph was taken (about 1920).

From studying census records we are fairly sure that Charles Samuel Ford was born on 2nd November 1870 to Fanny Ford, aged 18, unmarried and living with her parents in Cross Keys Yard. Also in the house was John Ford, born to Fanny's mother a month before her daughter gave birth. Soon after the 1971 census Fanny married Robert Shilton and by the time of the 1881 census the couple had 5 children plus Charles Samuel, now 10, and calling himself Charles Shilton. The Shiltons are recorded as living in Cross Keys Yard only 2 houses away from Fanny's parents. In 1891 the family are still in Cross Keys Yard but Charles Samuel Shilton/Ford does not appear to be in Atherstone, perhaps by the age of 21 he had already joined the military.

Charles next appears on December 25 1897 when he married Emily Agnes Gudger and when he seems to have reverted to his birth name of Ford, no father is named, just his mother, Fanny, so there is no doubt that it is the same man.

We can next trace Sam through the 1901 census when his wife Emily (Pem) Ford is living in Avins Yard and is listed as the Head of the household because she is the wife of a soldier serving in Africa. The photograph of granddad Sam in uniform fits in with the family recollections of him fighting in a war, it would appear that the war was the Boer War. Emily at this time had two sons, Charles 2 years old and 6 month-old Horace; sadly Horace died before his third birthday and is buried in Atherstone Cemetery.

In the 1911 census Charles is back with his family living in Richmond Road with his four surviving children, Charles, Sidney, Agnes and baby William. The grandchildren remember quite clearly visiting Grandma Pem and Grandpa Sam in one of the yards behind Harry Spittle's shoe shop but when and why they moved back into the town we don't know.

Sam died in 1957 followed by Emily in 1959.

CROWN YARD

Map Ref: 1	Yard No. 17	Long Street 44-46

First known in 1768 and inhabited intermittently until 1937.

Also known as **OLD CROWN YARD** in 1911 Census.

Clearance order made in 1935.

At the 1861 census both houses were uninhabited.

In 1901 1 house was occupied by a felt hat finisher with his wife and 4 children.

Herring Report listed 1 house and 2 children.

This yard had 2 houses with up to 6 people.

DOLPHIN YARD

Map Ref: 4	Yard No. 54	Long Street 162-164

First known in 1768 with 3 houses on this site and lived in continuously until 1934.

The houses in this yard were demolished in 1935 with the only tenant and family being displaced on 29th July to be re-housed in North Street.

A Clearance Order dated 19th January 1935 shows two dwelling houses together with 2 water closets and a partially demolished building owned by Strettons Brewery Co. Ltd.

The Census record of 1841 lists 8 houses in the Yard, with only 4 occupied. No records show more than 4 houses were ever occupied. The Clearance map for demolition shows four other buildings on the back of the Dolphin Pub still in existence, but presumably for pub use.

This yard had 4 houses with up to 12 people sharing a washhouse, a tap/pump and 2 privies.

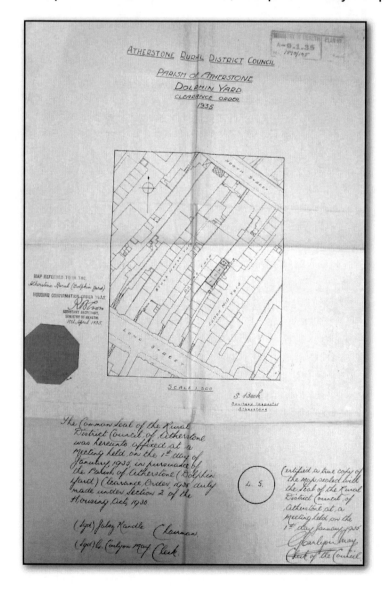

DRUIDS ARMS YARD

Map Ref: 9	Yard No. 129	Long Street 67-69

Built pre 1841.

Also known as **MARRIOTTS YARD** 1841.

Druids Yard was cleared in the Nelson Yard Clearance Scheme of 1926.

This yard had 13 houses with up to 65 people.

FACTORY YARD

Map Ref: 9	Yard No. 136	Long Street 63-65

In 1871 and 1881 census.

Also known as **HANDFORD YARD** 1851.

This yard had 5 houses.

FORDS YARD/BUILDINGS

Map Ref: 2	Yard No. 22	Long Street 64-66

In 1851 to 1901 census.

Also known as **WIMBURYS BUILDINGS 1911.**

The houses in this yard were demolished in 1937, though mentioned by Herring in his report of 1911.

This yard had 2 houses with up to 4 people sharing a tap/pump and 4 privies.

FOX YARD

Map Ref: 11	Yard No. 115	Coleshill Road

A reference point or image is not available.

This yard had 4 houses with up to 17 people.

This yard was off Coleshill Road and is not shown on the maps in this book.

First known in 1851.

From census records, the Fox, Foxes, or Fox's Yard was located on the Coleshill Road West, up between the Wharf, Queens Head and Maid of the Mill.

First listed in 1851 and known as Fox Yard. Containing 4 houses, the occupants of the 1st house are a Mr Joseph Fox (34) a bricklayer journeyman, his wife Rebecca (33) and their 6 children. The 4th house listed also has a William Henry Fox (24) and his wife Ann (28). He also is listed as a bricklayer journeyman.

By 1861 Foxes Yard is listed as containing 2 houses with 3 occupants, all listed as working within the hatting trade.

1871 and the yard no longer appears as such, but a Fox's Buildings is in the same location.

1881 and no yard or building works are listed.

1891 Foxes Yard reappears, containing 4 houses. Of the occupants listed, a Joseph Fox (74) a bricklayer and his wife Sarah (57), and their daughter Amelia (18) is working as a laundress. The next 2 houses contain people working in the hatting trade. The 4th house lists a widow and her sister, both working as laundresses.

From the census records, it appears Mr Joseph Fox had remarried and returned to the Yard many years after he first lived there.

FRIENDS MEETING HOUSE YARD

Map Ref: 5	Yard No. 57	Long Street 172-174

Only known from 1851 to 1871

This yard had 1 house with just one occupant, John Booth a 78 year old widowed pauper formerly a woolsorter from Leicestershire.

GARDEN ROW

Map Ref: 1	Yard No. 5	Long Street. 14-16

First known in 1831 and lived in continuously until 1965.

This yard had 13 houses with up to 51 people sharing 1 washhouse, a tap/pump and 4 privies.

The houses in this yard were demolished in 1965 and it was one of the last yards to go. The area covered by this yard, Rumseys Yard and Lagoes Buildings now contains the Library, Memorial Hall and Leisure Centre.

Life in Garden Row is well documented and still remembered in 2012.

This yard had 9 houses with up to 35 people living in the Yard.

In 1831 the houses were owned by Charles Holte Bracebridge of Atherstone Hall. The rent for each house was 2 shillings a week, which had to be paid every Monday morning. There were printed rules restricting to 3 the number of people who could use the wash house at any one time. Rainwater was to be used for washing and dirty water had to be disposed of other than by throwing it onto Long Street. He also set down rules about dealing with manure and rubbish and established rotas for cleaning the pump and privies. There was also land set aside for tenants to have a garden and Charles Wills Snr. won a medal for "most successful exhibitor" at Atherstone Horticultural Society Exhibition of 1894. held in the grounds of Merevale Hall. Charles Wills lived at number 13, which was slightly larger than the rest of the houses and he was the father of Charles Wills, the artist.

The Wills family are first recorded living at number 12 Garden Row in 1881 when Charles Wills Snr was recorded as living with his first wife, Louise. On the death of Louise, Charles married Hannah Spooner who had lodged with them.

Charles and Hannah went on to have seven children in the little house in Garden Row one of whom was Charles Wills, the artist. Their first born in 1883 was called Louisa , who later married and became Louisa Jephcott. The next two children were girls, Mary and Edith who went on to become Mrs. Morris and Mrs. Allsopp. When Edith was three, Charles William, was born on 28th February 1891 and there seems to have been a special bond between mother and son. Three more girls were born, Harriet (later Chetwynd), Alice and Dorothy, unfortunately Alice died aged 10 months in 1898 but Dorothy, who never married, was to be the person who shared her home with Charles in his later years and who was responsible for passing on her brother's work after his death.

GISBOURNES YARD

Map Ref: 7	Yard No. 82	Long Street 179-181

First known in 1861, lived in until 1936.

A Potters Yard is listed in 1768 with 1 house.

Also known as **POTTERS YARD** 1851 **LUCAS YARD** 1901

The houses in this yard were demolished by 1938 with many of the residents being re-housed in North Street.

A William Lucas, dairyman & greengrocer is listed as living at 181 Long Street in both the 1891 and 1901 census records and is likely to have given his name to this Yard for a short period of time before it reverted to Gisbournes Yard.

This yard had 2 houses with up to 13 people .

On the 1911 census both 179 and 181 Long Street are listed as shops. The former occupied by a Mr Lucas.

A list of values in respect of Yard properties from the early 1930's names a W.H.Charnell as the owner of two properties in Gisbournes Yard with a rateable value of £5 each.

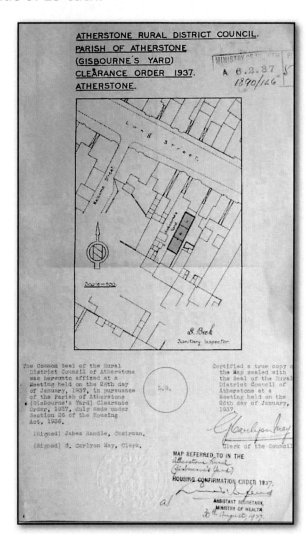

HADDON'S YARD

This yard had 3 houses with up to 5 people.

Map Ref: 11	Yard No. 116	Station Street

Only listed in 1851.

Haddons Yard only appeared on the 1851 census, containing 3 houses of which only 1 was occupied. Richard Smith and his wife Elizabeth and their grand-daughter Ann Taylor, they also had 2 lodgers – a hatter journeyman and an agricultural labourer.

HALLAMS YARD

THE BARBER SHOP

This yard had 7 houses with up to 32 people.

Map Ref: 7	Yard No. 85	Long Street 171-173

This yard does not appear until the 1901 census but is then on the electoral rolls until 1957.

Also known as **HALLAMS SQUARE**.

The houses in this yard were demolished in 1957.

Cynthia Challis and Pat Wileman recorded memories of living in this square at different times in the 1950s. They both remember Mrs Hunt's shop on the corner of Welcome Street opposite the Old Swan and how they took their ration books to her for sweets. The landlord was greengrocer, Bill Shilton and the rent was 7/6 a week. There were 4 houses down one side of the yard and 2 opposite with water obtained from a solitary tap. The houses were 'one up, one down' with a larder and a coal hole under the stairs which meant that coal had to be carried through the living room to be stored. Both remember the black leaded stove with a kettle always hanging on it, but the Challis house had theirs removed and a modern fire put in before they moved to Tudor Crescent in 1957.

Washday was a full day's job starting at 5 am when water was heated in the copper. On wet days the washing would be draped all round the house to dry. In the winter a kettleful of boiling water would have to be poured over the tap to thaw it out before starting to fill the copper. Pat Wileman moved to a new house in Mancetter.

HAND AND BOTTLE YARD

| Map Ref: 9 | Yard No. 125 | Long Street 81-83 |

Built pre 1841 lived in continuously until 1928.

Named after the public house that fronted the yard, the Hand and Bottle Yard has contained between 12 and 16 houses.

Situated on the south side of Long Street and running through to Station Street.

The Hand and Bottle Yard was one of those included in the Nelson Yard Clearance Scheme of 1928

1881 census. Sarah Miller (67) a former ribbon weaver is one of the residents. Under "where born", she is listed as "on the sea". From her age, we can put her as born in approximately 1814, so Sarah could possibly have been born on a ship during the Napoleonic War of 1803 – 1815.

This yard had 16 houses with up to 65 people.

1891 tells a tragic tale of one resident of the Yard. Mary Ann Hogg, a felt hat trimmer, originally from Birmingham. At just 30 years of age, she is a widow with 7 children ranging from 1 year to 14 years. Her 2 eldest daughters aged just 13 and 14 are having to work as an errand girl and mill girl respectively.

Map Ref: 4	Yard No. 37	Long Street 128-130

Built pre 1841 but known as the Hat and Beaver Yard from 1861 to 1936.

The houses in this yard were demolished in 1936.

In 1861 the licensee, George Shepherd had two trades, innkeeper and blacksmith. The Hat and Beaver public house is one of the few establishments in the town to take its name from the hatting trade, beaver fur being commonly used in the making of felt hats.

In the same 1861 census one of the cottages contained three generations of the same family comprising six adults and three small children all living in two small rooms.

This yard had 3 houses with up to 20 people sharing a tap/pump and 3 privies, although these may have been shared with the customers at the pub.

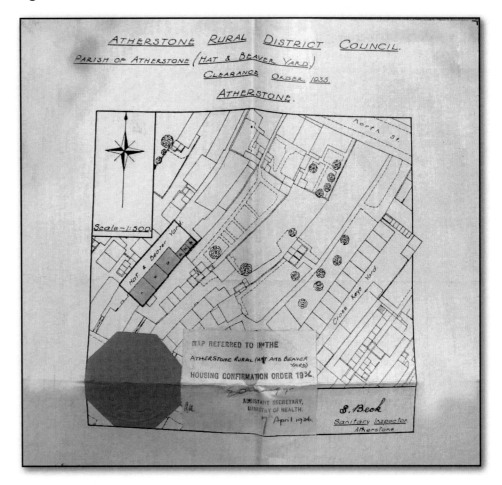

HATTONS YARD

Map Ref: 8	Yard No. 106	Long Street 113-115

First known in 1768 – 3 houses.

Recorded in the 1841, 1851 and 1911 census.

Also known as **GEES YARD** 1871.

This yard had 4 houses with up to 11 people.

HEATLES BUILDINGS

Map Ref: 7	Yard No. 80	Long Street 181-183

Only ever recorded in 1861.

Also known as **WHITES YARD** 1851.

This yard had 4 houses but only 1 was occupied.

HINCKS YARD

Map Ref: 8	Yard No. 104	Long Street 123-125

First known in 1768 up to demolition.

Date of demolition 1937.

This is a copy of the plan from a Clearance Order 1937 which lists 11 houses in the yard including three instances of two houses converted into one, together with one wash house, a rain water cistern, an ashpit and 8 water closets, all belonging to joint owners Rev Lester Charles Blower and Mrs William Clement Lambert.

The order also covered Nos. 10 and 12 South Street. The yard had access to both Long Street and South Street.

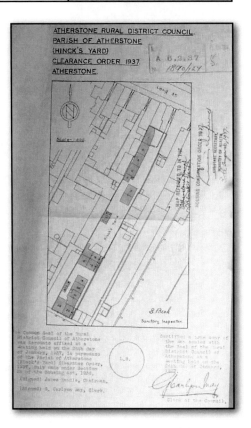

HUDSONS YARD

Map Ref: 4	Yard No. 47	Long Street 142-144

Built pre 1841 recorded in census in 1861 1881 and 1911.

Also known as **HATTONS YARD** 1911.

It is not known when the houses in this yard were demolished but they were on the list of yards suggested for demolition in the Herring Report of 1911. The yard was behind 142 and 144 Long Street which were described in a 1956 Demolition Order as being

"In an advanced state of dilapidations of walls, chimneys and roofs."

For some time after clearance this area was used as an open yard by Matthews butcher's shop at 148 Long Street. The butcher was licenced to kill his own meat and live animals were sometimes seen in this yard. It is now a small housing estate known as Tannery Close.

This yard had 4 houses with up to 7 people living there.

In the census of 1861 one of the houses in Hudsons Yard was occupied by George Warner, a blacksmith, who might well have carried out his trade in the yard.

INNAGE TERRACE

Map Ref: 11	Yard No. 119	Station Street

First known in 1861.

This yard was rebuilt about 1890 and is still occupied today (2012). At one time it backed onto the livestock market, now a car park.

JOHNSONS BUILDINGS

Map Ref: 10	Yard No. 155	Long Street 17-19 (Dem.)

Also known as **EARPS YARD** 1891.

It is not known when this house was demolished but it was one of the houses condemned in the Herring Report of 1911.

Tom Johnson bought Boss Yard in 1910. Johnson Buildings appear in 1911 census.

| Map Ref: 9 | Yard No. 127 | Long Street 73-75 |

Built pre 1841 and occupied continuously until 1928.

Another Yard named after the public house at its entrance, the Kings Arms pub was located on the site of the new arcade of shops on Long Street.

Over the decades, this Yard had contained between 13 and 17 houses, and several stables. The Kings Arms Yard became one of those destined for demolition under the Nelson Yard Clearance Scheme of 1928.

This yard had 16 houses with up to 73 people. The Yard had 5 middens and 2 ashpits.

As reported in the Atherstone News dated 5th June 1891, the Board of Guardians held a meeting in the Union Workhouse. Mr W.R.H. Chipperfield (Surveyor), presented his report. Amongst his recommendations for clearance he made a comment on the inadequate sanitary and building conditions in the Kings Arms Yard. He reported that 10 houses belonging to Mr Pettie's trustees, which house 54 people, have only 2 middens and 1 ashpit. A further 7 houses (4 of which are occupied, the other 3 are empty), belonging to Mrs Smalley, house 20 people, these have the use of 3 middens and 1 ashpit. The sanitary state of the Yard is reported as being in "a very bad condition", and found to be in a "very offensive state".

The yard also contained stables for several horses. The stables are described as being in a "dangerous condition". The walls have bulged and cracked and the floor above the stables is propped to prevent them from falling.

The paving in the Yard is also reported as being very bad in places.

He recommended that the owners be served notice to put in proper w.c.s and ashpits, to pave the yard where required and make the dangerous buildings safe.

Over a decade later, a notice of a property sale appears in the Atherstone News dated 26th September 1902. Lot 3 describes amongst other property, "9 houses in Kings Arms Yard and house fronting onto Station Street". These 10 houses are stated as bringing in an annual rental of £59.16s.

The auctioneer commented that it would be "a splendid opportunity for the town to purchase and make a side street of it", as the Yard runs through from Long Street to Station Street. Despite a number of bids received for these and several other properties in the Lot, the property was withdrawn at £750.

KITCHENS YARD

| Map Ref: 7 | Yard No. 96 | Long Street 149-151 |

First known in 1768 – 3 houses up to demolition.

Demolition

The houses in this yard were demolished in 1937.

This is a copy of the plan from the Housing Clearance Order 1937 for Kitchens Buildings listing 5 dwelling houses, an ash pit and two water closets. The owners are listed as Exors. James Kitchen (By subsequent purchase, Frank Coleman). The buildings to be vacated within four months.

Also known as
GAINS YARD 1851.

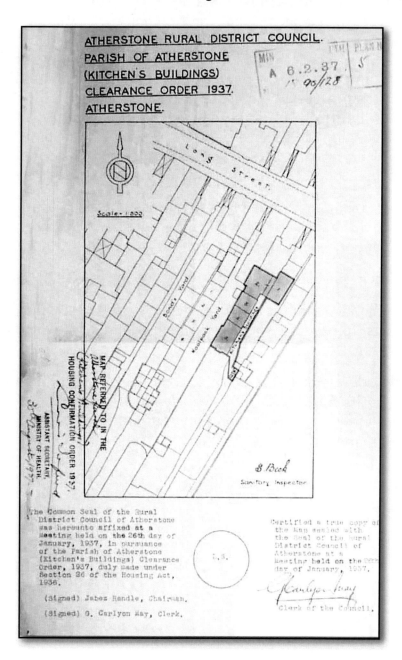

LAGOES BUILDINGS

Map Ref: 1	Yard No. 9	Long Street 20-26

First known in 1768 when there were 2 houses. Spelled LAGOS in 1871.

Occupied continuously to 1933 when staged demolition commenced.

The houses in this yard were finally demolished in 1965. The 1933 Clearance Scheme identified 2 houses with 18 occupants as needing rehousing. In 1935 another 8 houses were added to the list but from electoral roles we know that all 10 houses were still standing in 1965.

This yard had 10 houses with up to 35 people.

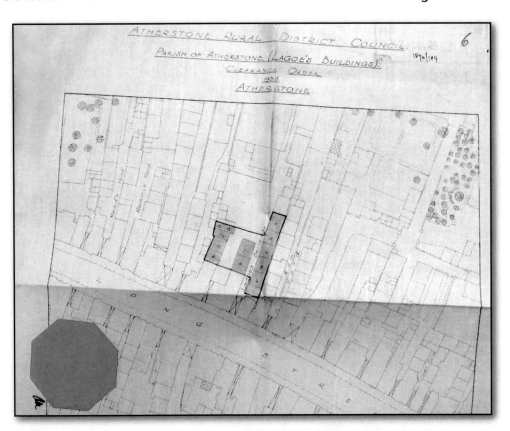

MAYS YARD

Map Ref: 4	Yard No. 50	Long Street 150-152

This yard only appears on the Herring Report 1911.

This yard had 2 houses with up to 10 people living there.

MEADS YARD

Map Ref: 1	Yard No. 3	Long Street 8-10

One house recorded in 1768 occupied by Samuel Orton. Also known as **ORTONS YARD** 1841 to 1911 but called **MEADS YARD** in 1911.

Three of the houses in this yard were condemned in 1936 and the owners were given to the end of 1937 to have their properties demolished. In the 1990s the site was used as a car repair garage and in 2007 a new house was built on the land facing onto Croft Road.

Although in the 1911 census it was known as Meads Yard, most of the tales about it refer to the area as Ortons Yard. At one time there was a butcher's shop on the front and the butcher would buy cattle at the market and walk them round to the yard for slaughter. If a beast was particularly big it would not fit down the narrow alley so the butcher would slaughter it on Long Street and take it through in joints of beef.

This yard had 4 houses with up to 18 people.

MERCERS YARD/BUILDINGS

This yard had 5 houses with up to 20 people.

Map Ref: 5	Yard No.74	Long Street 202-204

First known in 1901.

Also known as **PAYNES BUILDINGS** 1881-91 possibly **FARMERS YARD** 1841, **BARSBYS YARD** in Herring Report 1911.

There is a Clearance Order for 3 dwelling houses and a washhouse dated 6 February 1937 owned by a Mr Harry Lucas, who owned 5 houses in this Yard. Two houses were still on the Electoral Roll in 1965.

There is a Farmers Yard listed on the 1841 census with two of three houses occupied. A James Farmer, gardener, is the previous entry and may have given name to the Yard. This Yard does not appear again but we believe to be on the same site as Mercers Yard.

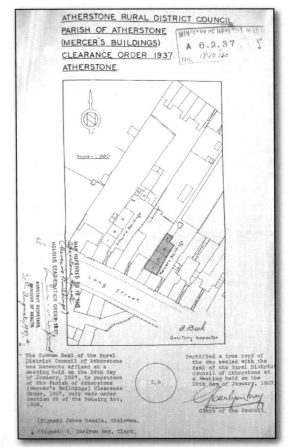

MILLERS YARD

This yard had 2 houses with up to 4 people living there.

Map Ref: 3	Yard No. 29	Long Street 94-96

Built pre 1841, last recorded in 1851.

MILLS YARD

Map Ref: 5	Yard No. 65	Long Street 186-188

Only appears on 1841 and 1851 census records.

On both census records the previous entry to Mills Yard show an Elizabeth Mills.

Samuel Beale, a journeyman hatter, and his family together with an Elizabeth Beale, a ribbon weaver, with her family both lived in this Yard. It is possible, looking at ages, that Elizabeth is Samuel's mother.

MOUNT PLEASANT YARD

Map Ref: 5	Yard No. 64	Long Street 178-180

First date known 1768 with 4 houses.

Also known as **GOTHARDS YARD** in 1851.

The houses in this yard were demolished after 1960.

In 1891 we find Alfred George Fox with his wife and family at 180 Long Street as a Bracebridge tenant. Alfred like his father, who put up many of the yards and factories, was a general builder and converted the bottom of the garden into his building yard. His son Fletcher, a journeyman joiner is living at 178 on the 1901 census. Alfred continued the building of the North Street Schools on his father's death and built some of Atherstone's first modern terraces beyond South Street.

This yard had 6 houses with up to 37 people in 1881

Alfred was followed by his son Reginald, usually known as Rex, who in turn built on the North Street Council Estate. In 1931 after 40 years of Fox tenancy the Bracebridge entail was lifted and Rex was able to buy the entire property of two half and a quarter burgage plots.

Rex's daughter Mary was to become an accomplished artist, who exhibited widely both at home and abroad.

In 1956 Mrs Fox sold number 180 and later the builders yard and Mount Pleasant as separate lots.

Although it had only one entrance into the Yard, Dr Herring in his report recognised that Mount Pleasant lived up to its name, being one of only three yards he considered having 'a fair amount of open space'.

| Map Ref: 9 | Yard No. 126 | Long Street 75-77 |

First known in 1768 – 3 houses and lived in continuously until 1928.

The houses in this yard were demolished under the Nelson Yard Clearance Scheme.

The Nelson Yard Clearance Scheme highlighted a total of 5 yards running between Long Street and Station Street for demolition. These adjacent yards were Druids Arms Yard; Hand & Bottle Yard; Kings Arms Yard; Nelson Yard and Spencer's Yard.

The Nelson Yard Slum Clearance Scheme commenced in 1926 and was completed by the summer of 1929 at a cost of £32,233. New houses were being built in New Road and Westwood Road and around 350 people were rehoused in 70 new houses.

From an article in the Atherstone News dated 26th September 1902 (see quote under Kings Arms Yard), where it is hinted at the opportunity to provide a new side street running from Long Street to Station Street, this Site Clearance would seem ideal given the proximity of Church Street on the opposite side of Long Street, to enable traffic access to Station Street.

This yard had up to 14 houses with up to 62 people.

OLD HOUSE YARD

| Map Ref: 8 | Yard No. 103 | Long Street 127-129 |

First date known: 1911.

OLD HOUSE YARD 2

| Map Ref: 10 | Yard No. 160 | Long Street 13-15 Dem. |

First known in 1768 and lived in until 1911.

A reference point or image is not available.

This yard had 5 houses.

OLD PLOUGH YARD

Map Ref: 4	Yard No. 40	Long Street 134-136

First known in 1768.

Also known as **ELLIS YARD** 1841 **WRIGHTS YARD** 1851 **OLD PLOUGH YARD** 1861 to 1937

All but one of the houses in this yard were demolished in 1937 despite being on the list for demolition in the Herring Report of 1911.

The census of 1861 is worth studying for this yard because it was then at its most overcrowded.

This yard had 4 houses with up to 25 people sharing a tap/pump and 3 privies. There was also a separate coal house.

One house contained just an elderly couple, Ambrose Hatton, a hatter and his wife. John Fox, a baker, and his wife, shared the next house with their five children. Next door was occupied by the Lawtons, husband, wife and six children while the final dwelling housed Charles Beck, his wife, a teenaged son and daughter along with a married daughter, her husband and their two-year-old son. A total of 25 people aged from 72 to 1 living in four small houses.

ORMES YARD

Map Ref: 2	Yard No. 27	Church Street

Only ever recorded in 1861.

This yard had 1 house with up to 3 people.

PAYNES YARD

Map Ref: 4	Yard No. 53	Long Street 160-162

Built prior to 1841 and lived in continuously until 1934.

Also known as **SMITHS YARD** 1841 – 1871.

The houses in this yard were due for demolition in 1935. At one time an above ground open-air swimming pool was built in the space, now it houses the Guide hut.

By 1958 there was only one house still lived in. Walter Bown was married to a Leicester girl and they had a small child but she lived with her parents in Leicester and Walter lived with his aunt in Paynes Yard. Eventually Mrs Bown moved with the baby to be with her husband but her new doctor said the house was not fit for a baby. She went to see the Medical Officer at the Council and was told that she had no right coming into the town expecting to be housed! However, a few weeks later, they were re-housed in Lister Road.

This yard had 9 houses sharing 2 washhouses, a tap/pump and 4 privies.

This is just one of many stories told of how people moved into the yard houses, despite their dilapidated condition, in order to be re-housed in the new houses being built for that purpose.

PAYNES LODGING HOUSE YARD

Map Ref: 6	Yard No. 78	Long Street 189-191

Built prior to 1841 and occupied until 1911.

Condemned as unfit by the Herring Report of 1911.

Located next door to the Workhouse.

PEARMANS YARD

Map Ref: 5	Yard No. 70	Long Street 200-202

Probably built before 1841, it was inhabited until 1939.

Also known as **VINRACES YARD** 1841 and **MILLERS YARD** 1891.

Pearmans was variously spelt Permains and Pearmans and has been found mentioned in 1924-1939.

A James Miller, photographer, lived at the top of the yard in 1891 and may have given his name to the yard at that time.

PHOENIX YARD

Map Ref: 2	Yard No. 24	Church Street

First known in 1768 - with 2 houses lived in continuously until 1959.

Also known as **SIMMONDS YARD** in 1861 census.

The houses in this yard were partially demolished in 1937.

From the 1861 census – 10 houses inhabited, age of occupants from 12 months to 81 years – the 81 year old still working as a maltster.

Occupations have included Chelsea Pensioner 67 and wife 45, a charwoman, hatters, tailors, dressmaker, cordwainer, farm labourer, railway porter, painters apprentice.

This yard had 15 houses with up to 73 people sharing 1 washhouse, 1 tap and 4 water closets.

At the hearing to discuss the proposed Clearance Order a Mrs Alice Eliza Ward owned 10 houses: 5 with living room and 2 bedrooms, 3 had a living room and 1 bedroom, 1 had a living room, scullery and 2 bedrooms, and 1 had 2 living rooms and 2 bedrooms. They were so close together, they were equivalent to 88 houses to the acre as opposed to 12 to the acre under the draft Town Planning Scheme.

There were 4 w.c.s and 1 washhouse attached at one end of the yard – some distance for those at the other end, and one tap in the middle of the yard. The defects included: general dampness, no through ventilation, adequate supply of water not readily available, as was the washing accommodation and provision of w.c..s.. Inadequate drainage or sanitary sinks, no satisfactory food store. Further contraventions of bye-laws included: lack of open space at the rear, height of rooms, absence of concrete subfloor, no damp course, windows too small.

Additionally the structure was in poor order, with tie bars in places and brickwork bulging badly. Internal condition very poor and coal kept in the understairs cupboard.

The Herring Report, noted 13 houses occupied by 35 adults and 23 children.

PINCHBECKS YARD

| Map Ref: 3 | Yard No. 31 | Long Street 100-102 |

Listed in 1861 only.

Also known as **MUSTONS YARD** in 1851.

It is not known when this house was demolished, it may have reverted to being a storeroom or shed. In 1861 there must have been an arrangement between the owner of the house on Long Street, John Pinchbeck, and William Meadows and his wife to allow them to live in his yard. By 1871, when the next census was taken, William and Matilda, with their growing family, had moved to Ansley village and Pinchbecks Yard is no longer listed. However, Ann Pinchbeck, John's widow, is still recorded as living on Long Street at the entrance to Pinchbecks Yard.

This yard had 1 house containing 3 people.

By chance, in Warwick Record Office, our researchers found a copy of John Pinchbeck's will. He had died in 1870 and left his wife "seven cottages and shops in the Kings Arms Yard". The rents from these properties would have allowed Ann to live independently, or they could have attracted 'gold-digging' suitors. By searching through subsequent censuses we have been able to follow Ann right through until her death in 1886 at the age of 70. She had never re-married but had shared her home with three of her daughters, Sarah, Lucy and Kate all described as unmarried teachers. Sarah became the Head of a Ladies School and in the 1881 census mother and three daughters have moved to a house in North Street. All three daughters are recorded as dying in Atherstone aged 76, 79 and 82 years respectively and all remained unmarried.

PITTAMS YARD

| Map Ref: 5 | Yard No. 67 | Long Street 196-198 |

Built pre 1841 known as Pittams 1851-1891 and 1911 to demolition.

Also known as **ORTONS YARD** 1841 and **COPES YARD** 1901.

The houses in this yard were demolished in 1938 with many of the residents being re-housed in North Street.

The 1937 Clearance Order lists 3 dwelling houses, a washhouse and 2 water closets owned by a Mrs Amy Hannah Brown.

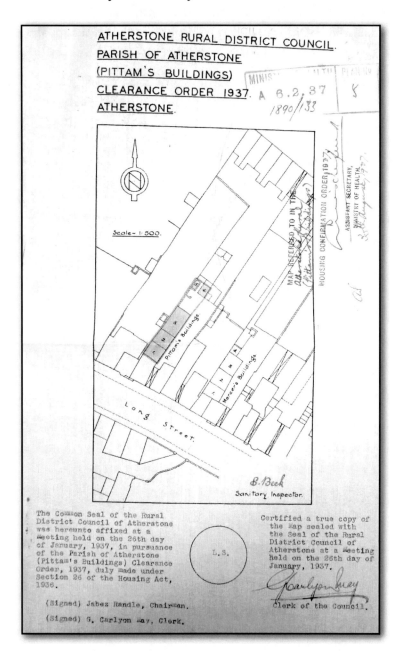

This yard had 4 houses with up to 13 people sharing a washhouse and 2 privies.

RADFORDS BUILDING/YARD

Map Ref: 7	Yard No. 94	Long Street 163-165

Built pre 1841.

Also known as **KENT YARD** 1841 - 1861.

This yard had 2 houses with up to 9 people sharing.

RADFORD YARD

Map Ref: 8	Yard No. 108	Long Street 109-111

Only appears in the census for 1891.

Also known as **EVERETTS YARD** 1841.

This yard had 2 houses with up to 4 people sharing.

RAILWAY TAVERN YARD

A reference point or image is not available.

This yard had only 1 house with 5 people.

Map Ref: 10	Yard No. 163	Long Street demolished

Only known in 1851.

It is not known when this yard was demolished.

In 1851 Mr and Mrs Sketchley and their 3 young children were the only residents in the yard.

RAM YARD

Map Ref: 1	Yard No. 11	Long Street 28-30

First known in 1768 – 3 houses.

Also known as **WHITES COURT** 1841.

The census records, show only 1 house with at the most 3 people in it, yet this early photograph shows quite a large group of children. It may be that the house on the right of the wall is Ram Yard and where the children are is Lagos Buildings, which had 10 houses, or the photograph may be wrongly labelled.

The houses in this yard were demolished in 1965 to make way for the building of the Library.

RICHMOND HILL YARD

Map Ref: 11	Yard No. 114	Coleshill Road

Only ever recorded in 1861.

Richmond Hill Yard appears only once in 1861. Located up by Gas House Yard, off the Coleshill Road West.

Containing just 2 houses yet occupied by 13 people (plus 1 visitor), both heads of the houses work for the railway. Mr Richard Pratt is a railway porter and his neighbour Mr John Dawson is a railway labourer.

ROES YARD

Map Ref: 10	Yard No. 140	Station Street

Probably built earlier but only recorded in 1841 and 1851

It is not known when the houses were demolished.

ROGERS BUILDINGS/YARD

Map Ref: 1	Yard No. 16	Long Street 34-36

First known in 1768 – 3 houses.

Also known as **MUSTONS YARD** 1841 and **ROES YARD** 1851 1861.

This yard had 2 houses with up to 16 people.

RUMSEYS YARD

Map Ref: 1	Yard No. 4	Long Street 10-12

Built pre 1841.

Three houses in this yard were due for demolition in 1936 but they were eventually cleared in 1965.

This yard had 5 houses with up to 16 people.

These houses were described as having 1 room on the ground floor with a bedroom and a landing bedroom upstairs.

SALES YARD/BUILDINGS

Map Ref: 7	Yard No. 92	Long Street 167-169

This yard had 10 houses with up to 28 people sharing a washhouse, and 4 privies.

First known in 1768 – 2 houses to demolition.

Other names with dates **BIDDLES YARD** 1851 and **MOUSLEYS YARD** 1841.

Date of demolition 1937 - 4 houses including house fronting Long Street.

1957 - 7 dwellings.

1st December 1936 Resolution passed declaring specified area to be a clearance area.

26th January 1937 Clearance Order made and submitted to Minister of Health for confirmation.

30th August 1937 Ministry of Health confirms Order for demolition of 4 dwelling houses, 1 wash house and 2 coal houses owned by the Exors Alfred Sale with 4 month's notice to vacate the buildings.

This includes a dwelling house fronting Long Street.

A report compiled by The Chief Public Health Inspector Mr Acton dated 14th November 1956 gives a brief description of the premises in the 'Sales and Simond's Building Clearance Order.' 1956.

The two blocks of cottages face each other with the distance between being 14 feet. All the dwellings have just a living room with an unsatisfactory pantry off, with a steep winding 'private' bedroom off. The coal places are underneath the staircases. There is no water supply and no sink in the houses, instead all share a mains water standpipe in front of no. 4.

There is rising damp and all suffer from open jointed brickwork, perished mortar and defects of floors, walls ceilings and woodwork.

Two wash houses and one wash line attached to the gable wall of no. 7 are used by all seven tenants. Six families share 3 of a block of 4 water closets leaning to the gable of no. 1 whilst the family in no. 5 have the private use of the fourth.

Pathways are in a poor condition as is the channel for slop and storm water drainage.

Mr Acton states 'I am of the opinion that all the above referred to houses are until for human habitation and that the most satisfactory method of dealing with the conditions is the demolition of all the buildings in this area.'

SIMONDS YARD/BUILDINGS

Map Ref: 7	Yard No. 89	Long Street 167-169

First known in 1768 – 2 houses.

Also known as **CORBETTS YARD** 1841 1861 1871 **HULLS YARD** 1841 1851 1861 1881 **HADDONS YARD** 1851 1871.

This seems to be one of those yards sharing a common entrance but having different names for different parts.

Some of the houses in these yards were demolished in 1937 but there were still people on the Electoral Roll in 1957. There was a corner shop on this site until the 1960s when the whole area was cleared to build flats and row of shops with maisonettes above.

SPENCERS YARD/BUILDINGS

Map Ref: 9	Yard No. 133	Long Street 67-69

First known in 1768 – 1 house.

Also known as **PARTRIDGES YARD** 1911 **BARNES YARD** 1891 **LLOYDS YARD** 1841.

This yard had 6 houses with up to 25 people. It shared an entrance with Druids Arms Yard and was separated from it by a wall.

The houses in this yard were demolished in 1926, although there were still people giving this as an address in the Electoral Roll for 1959.

SPENCER'S YARD

This yard had 1 house with 5 people.

Map Ref: 10	Yard No. 157	Long Street 17 – 19

Only listed in 1841 and 1851.

Not to be confused with another Spencers Yard on Long Street.

The residents at the time of the census are an Ann Randall, a widowed laundress, who lives with her daughter and son-in-law and her 2 grand-children.

STANTONS BUILDINGS

This yard had 1 house with 5 people.

Map Ref: 5	Yard No. 75	Long Street 202-204

Only recorded in 1871.

STEVENSONS YARD

| Map Ref: 8 | Yard No. 112 | Long Street 109-111 |

First known in 1768 – 2 houses.

Also known as **BASSETTS YARD** 1841 **SANDS YARD** 1851 **HAMBREYS YARD** 1861 1871.

Date of demolition: 1956.

Oral History. Mr Arthur Johnson: "I was born in Stevensons Place which he recollects was opposite the old post office, which is TNT offices nowadays. Stevensons Place was between Binleys which was a kind of greengrocers and Harry Spittles which was a shoe shop."

This yard had 7 houses with up to 28 people sharing 4 privies and 2 wash houses.

Map Ref: 9	Yard No. 139	Long Street 49-51

First known in 1768 – 1 house. Recorded as being inhabited from 1841 to 1957.

Also known as **ROGERS YARD** 1911.

This yard had up to 9 houses with up to 24 people sharing a washhouse, a tap/ pump and 3 privies.

Date of demolition: 1958.

Reduced from 9 houses and 5 people on 1956 Electoral Roll to 2 people in 1 house in 1957. One house had been vacant for approximately 10 years.

Demolition order made in 16 July 1956. All houses being considered unstable; poor natural light; unsatisfactory ventilation.

In 1901 Mary Pepper and her sister Flora aged 16, and 15 with the occupation of shoe finishers are stated as not knowing where they were born. They were sent from London as children to be boarded out.

Earlier History – in 1650 Joan Taylor, a widow, was living here but by 1660 the premises had come into the hands of the Drayton family. By 1747 it was owned by Joseph Steele with five dwellings; by 1793 there were also two hatters' workshops. Late in 1825 the premises comprised the Swan and Two Necks Inn and a butcher's shop. There were 8 dwellings.

In 1831 Joseph Willday was the owner; by then there were six dwellings, three hatters' finishing shops and a stable in the yard. By 1851 all heads of households in the 6 dwellings were hatters.

SWAN YARD

Map Ref: 3	Yard No. 28	North Street

First known in 1841, last known in 1861.

The Swan Yard was to the right through the arch in the Market Place. It is recorded in three censuses 1841, 51 and 61 when the same three families were resident. John Bates, a farmer, Joseph Fox, a bricklayer and Rebecca Allen, a milk seller. In the 1871 census the yard has disappeared with only Rebecca Allen remaining a few houses down North Street as housekeeper to a solicitor. The archway was constructed in the 1790s to divert the road from going behind St. Mary's Church and in front of Atherstone Hall. At some stage after this the Swan Inn became the home to a series of doctors and their families and eventually became Atherstone Surgery.

This yard had 3 houses with up to 9 people living in it.

T VEROS YARD

Map Ref: 9	Yard No. 128	Long Street demolished

Only recorded in the 1891 census.

The Land accessed through Druids Arms Yard from Long Street may have also had an entrance on Station Street. The yards in the area that is now Atherstone's bus station was densely packed with tiny houses and distinguishing one from the other is almost impossible. T Veros Yard was one of those yards.

This yard had 8 houses with up to 47 people.

TATES YARD

Map Ref: 10	Yard No. 162	Station Street

First known in 1768 – 2 houses but not mentioned after 1851.

It is not known when the houses were demolished.

Only appears in 1841 and 1851 census. Most families in this yard had four or five children.

This yard had up to 13 houses with up to 58 people.

THROWERS YARD

Map Ref: 1	Yard No. 8	Long Street 20-22

This yard is only recorded on the 1851 and 1861 censuses

It is not known why it ceased to be inhabited.

VEROS YARD

Map Ref: 10	Yard No. 161	Long Street 9-11 Dem.

First known in 1841 and occupied continuously until 1957 despite being condemned by Herring in 1911.

The houses in this yard were demolished in 1958.

There were 6 houses with 13 people in 1957.

Life in this yard

In 1901 more coal miners were living in Atherstone. There were 3 underground workers in this yard.

A reference point or image is not available.

This yard had 6 houses with up to 31 people.

VEROS YARD/TERRACE

Map Ref: 10	Yard No. 150	Long Street 25-27

First known in the 16th century but only listed in 1901.

Also known as **ROADKNIGHTS YARD** 1851.

The houses in this yard were demolished in 1958.

Life in this yard

A large plot of ¾ burgage which belonged to the Drayton family, tanners from 16th century. Michael Drayton, 1563-1631, was part of this large family, who owned property in Atherstone and London. Thomas Freer bought the property in 1712 and continued tanning on the site. By 1825, William Freer shared the premises with John Roberts, who had a stable and pig sty. By 1851 this was known as Roadknights Yard, occupied by Catherine Hargrave, 62, a widow and her grand-daughter Kitty Banks, 10 ,born in Tucking Field, Cheshire. Catherine had a daughter also named Catherine, 23, who in 1848 had a whirlwind romance and married James Roper, a printer from Essex. Within two months of their marriage, the couple had emigrated to Australia.

This yard had 8 houses with up to 18 people.

VINRACES ROW

Map Ref: 3	Yard No. 32	Long Street 118-120

First known in 1768 – 4 houses.

The houses in this yard were demolished in 1959 although it had been earmarked for clearing in Dr. Herring's report published in 1911.

Although the houses appear to be the usual one-up-one-down variety, seven of them had a small garden with a shed so had a much more open aspect at the front, although they backed directly onto a hat factory. In 1861 heads of households were skilled workers, a lawyer, two grooms, a taylor and a coachmaker indicating that it was perhaps a more expensive yard in which to live.

This yard had up to 9 houses with up to 21 people sharing 2 washhouses, a tap/ pump and 3 privies.

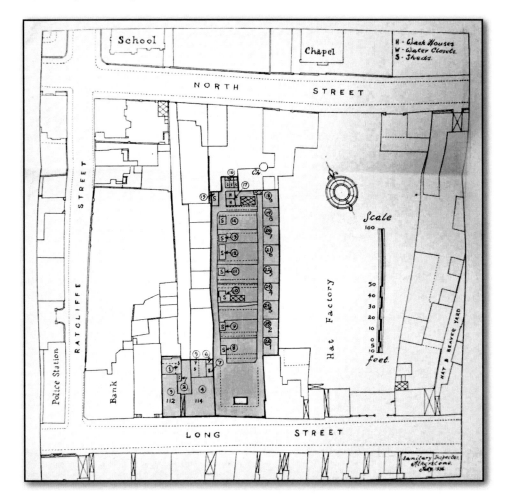

WASH PAD YARD

Map Ref: 10	Yard No. 164	Station Street

First known in 1768 when Mr Noon owned 2 houses. Only recorded on the census of 1851.

Only appear in 1851 census when the two heads of household and their wives both worked in the hatting industry.

This yard had 7 houses with up to 30 people.

WHEATSHEAF YARD

Map Ref: 10	Yard No. 149	Long Street 29-31

First known in 1768.

Wheatsheaf Yard does not appear in the census after 1901. This property was also owned by the Drayton's in the 17th Century. Thomas Hill, a cordwainer, lived there until his death in 1719. An inventory at his death showed brewing utensils and a shovel board suggesting the building was used as an inn. Joseph Adouck who owned the premises in 1746 was a victualler. By 1825 there were 5 tenements in the yard behind the inn and two hatters shops. In 1851 there were seven of which four heads of households were hatters. There was also a hatters shop, a stable, a pigsty and a "necessary house". In 1876 there were eight cottages.

This yard had 5 houses with up to 13 people with 1 privy.

WHITBYS YARD

Map Ref: 3	Yard No. 33	Long Street 122-124

First known in 1841, recorded until 1871.

It is not known when the houses in this yard were demolished or why they do not appear on the census after 1871 but they were listed for demolition in the Herring Report of 1911.

In 1851 James Batty, a 20 year old living in this yard was listed as being a railway porter. He must have been one of the first porters to serve at Atherstone Station as the railway line only opened in December 1847.

This yard had 9 houses with up to 32 people living there.

WHITE BEAR YARD

Map Ref: 1	Yard No. 12	Long Street 30-32

First known in 1841.

Also known as **FRIARS YARD** 1861.

The houses in this yard were demolished in 1965 when the space became a car park serving the pub. Although called the 'White Bear' locals always referred to this establishment as 'The Clock' for obvious reasons.

This yard had 3 houses with up to 17 people.

WHITE HART YARD

Map Ref: 1	Yard No. 1	Long Street

Built pre 1841.

The stables in this yard were converted to houses in the 1990s, prior to that they had been used as storage and garages. In the 1960s the Atherstone branch of motorbike 'Rockers' were allowed to meet in the yard.

The pub itself was first a coaching inn then a commercial hotel catering for rail travellers. In the 19th century regular auctions were advertised in the yard ranging from second hand furniture to livestock. In an advertisement dated 1900 the White Hart advertised "oysters fresh from the coast" and owners of houses in Croft Road at the end of the yard still dig up oyster shells in their gardens.

This yard had 1 house with up to 4 people living in it.

WHITE LION YARD

Map Ref: 11	Yard No. 117	Station Street

First listed in 1841 and lived in until 1959.

Located to the rear of the White Lion public house (which still bears the same name today), the White Lion Yard is consistent in always having 5 houses, from the 1851 census records up to 1938. The highest occupancy of the Yard was 32 people in 5 houses in 1891.

Mr Joe Smith gives his recollections in an oral history, some of which are set out below.

Joe and his parents moved into number 3 White Lion Yard in 1938. He recalls there being 5 houses in a row, with a toilet to the left at the far end of the Yard, along with a washhouse and 1 tap to supply all 5 houses, with a drain at the entrance to the Yard.

The first house in the Yard was occupied by Fred White and his wife Kitty, they didn't have any children.

At number 2 lived Mrs Simpson and her son Charlie. Described as a very old lady, Charlie is described as being a grown up man, as old as Joe's own father. He was an ex Guardsman and a miner. Shortly after Joe moved in, Mrs Simpson died. Charlie got married and moved to Polesworth.

No 3 was occupied by a gentleman called Sid Beale with 5 children. New houses were being completed in Bank Road and the family were allocated one of these houses due to overcrowding.

At number 4 lived a gentleman called Bert Heptinstall, described as a tiny man at only 5 feet tall, Joe says as a kid he was the same size as him. His brother who lived in Nottingham came to visit him and Joe found it amusing that he dressed in "breeches and leather riding gaiters", but he wasn't a farmer!

At the far end of the Yard at number 5 lived Danny Cook, his wife Florrie and their 5 children. At the bottom of the Yard on the left was a house that backed onto the sweet shop at the front, run by a spinster Nancy Allsop. This house wasn't classed as being in White Lion Yard. It was occupied by Sam and Kitty Barlow and their 2 children.

The houses in the Yard were owned by the publican of the White Lion Inn, Henry Beale. His brother Sid had lived at number 3 White Lion Yard. Henry Beale had inherited the pub and houses from his father, which Joe believes were "shared up between the brothers".

Describing his house, Joe recalls the chimneys were joined to the house next door, so could be on the left or right hand side. There was an old fashioned range, quite a wide fireplace, a mantelpiece that he estimates as being 4 and a half foot to 5 foot high, the width being 5 to 6 foot.

This yard had 5 houses with up to 32 people sharing 1 washhouse, a tap and 1 privy.

A range was set in an alcove in the chimney breast with an old fashioned hob on the left hand side, being about 18 inches to 2 foot. Underneath there was a little door that lifted off to clear the soot out of the grate. Joe describes black leading the range as being useful training for when you went in the army, spit and polishing your boots! Over the fireplace was a little door about a foot wide by about 6 inches, that would flap down to rest a saucepan on.

Over the fireplace was a swivel device, described as similar to a hanging basket bracket, that could swing over the fireplace or fold back onto the range, being about 15 inches long with a series of holes like a belt buckle. This had various implements hanging off it, like a stew pot. In front of the fire was a fender to keep the children from standing too close too the fire.

Wednesday was Joe's mothers wash day. He describes how all the ladies in the yard had their own dollies hung up at the back of the washhouse, and their own props. After doing the laundry, his mother would bail some buckets out of the tub, pouring it into the drain at the front of the yard. When there was only 4 or 5 inches of water left, she would roll the barrel into the house and pour the water into the bathtub, each of the children would have a bath in succession, then she would roll the tub back into the washhouse, cleaning the washhouse for the next person.

In winter, the houses would take it in turns to thaw the tap in the yard by pouring boiling water over it.

The toilet is described as being an old fashioned type with a cast iron tank on the wall. The door was ill fitting with a large gap at the top and bottom, with a hole about 15 inches square over the door, with no glass in it. As Joe says "you didn't hang about!".

WILDAYS YARD

Map Ref: 10	Yard No. 141	Long Street 37-39

First known in 1768 – 3 houses.

Also known as **BINGHAMS YARD** 1841-1901.

Appears as Wildays from 1911 census until the houses in this yard were demolished starting in 1935.

The reasons for demolition cited: Lack of ventilation, scullery sinks, drainage. Inadequate food storage, washing facilities in disrepair. No water laid on to washhouses. Communal drain running down yard.

This yard in 1935 had 22 houses, 112 people and 3 wash houses.

Dr Fisher gave evidence in the enquiry.

These houses were also the back to back type.

This yard was owned by Mr G F Collins, a Grocer and Tea-merchant.

He objected to the order, stating that he would lose the greater part of his income, if the houses were demolished. He added that this would be hard because he was 75 and he had invested the bulk of his savings into the property and he now realised his mistake.

In a report in Atherstone News 29 September 1933 it was stated that it was the congestion of the houses which caused the problem. Mr Hatton the Chairman said that all the houses would not be demolished in one year, but would be spread over five years.

The Baddesley pit disaster of 1882 took the lives of 32 men most of whom lived around the mine at Baxterley and Baddesley.

Just 2 Atherstone men lost their lives and they both lived in Binghams Row (*the yard under the present Aldi shop*). This was the most over-crowded yard in the town with a population density greater than the most crowded of Birmingham's slum dwellings.

This photograph is of Emma Archer of Bingham's Row and her five children taken in 1885. *(Thanks to Stan Archer)*

Emma's husband, Richard, was one of the Atherstone men involved in the pit disaster and, although he was rescued alive and taken home, he finally succumbed to his injuries 2 months later, on June 29th 1882. Imagine nursing a man with severe burns in one of the tiny houses in Bingham's Row whilst looking after five children under the age of 11!

A quick look through the Census forms shows that Emma went on to marry William Archer, her husband's cousin, in 1883 and together they had Emma 1885, Maud 1888, Richard 1894, Alfred 1897 and Beatrice 1900 – a total of 10 children. In 1901 Emma and William had moved back to Grendon with eight of their children, the older ones having left home to work, Joseph living on a farm in Sheepy and William serving as a baker on Long Street, Atherstone.

Emma died in 1939 aged 86, three months after her husband, William. Sadly burial records also record that while she lived in Bingham's Row Emma lost 3 children in infancy. *Celia Parton provided this information.*

WINTERS YARD/TERRACE

| Map Ref: 8 | Yard No. 113 | Long Street 103-105 |

First known in 1768 – 2 houses and lived in continuously until 1957.

By a resolution passed on 18th June 1956, the Council declared this area so defined to be a Clearance Area.

A further resolution on 17th September 1956 ordered the demolition of the buildings, which consisted of 3 waterclosets, a washhouse and 3 dwelling houses in Winters Terrace owned by the Atherstone Industrial Co-operative Society.

From House Inspection Records dated 9th February 1956, we know that all three tenants had lived in the same houses for over 20 years and that at the time of inspection, were paying 8 shillings & six pence a week in rent.

A total of 9 adults and 4 children are listed.

2 hat factory workers, 4 colliery workers, 2 Merevale laundry women and 1 other.

Two houses were, 2 up 2 down. One had an additional small bedroom.

All 3 shared one washhouse in the yard and were at least 22 yards from the water closet with one house 33 yards away.

All 3 houses by this time did have a tap over a white glazed sink placed in the scullery or food store.

All 3 heads of household expressed a wish to leave.

This yard had 3 houses with up to 14 people sharing a washhouse, and 3 privies.

WOODMAN YARD

Map Ref: 10	Yard No. 148	Station Street

First date known 1911.

The houses in this yard were demolished in 1936. House Confirmation Order 1936.

This yard had 2 houses. It was named after the Woodman public house which survived into the 1950s.

WOODS YARD

| Map Ref: 9 | Yard No. 124 | Long Street 83-85 |

Built prior to 1841, occupied until 1928.

Also known as **GUTTERIDGES YARD** 1841 1851.

ASHERS YARD 1871.

Woods Yard was located off Long Street and today the entrance still exists as a walk through to Station Street. Known as Gutteridges Yard from census records in 1841 and 1851, with 3 houses and 13 occupants. By 1861 the Yard was known as Ashers Buildings, thereafter in 1871 Asher's Yard. By 1881 the Yard was renamed Wood's Yard and kept the name in the 1891, 1901 and 1911 census records.

This yard had 5 houses with up to 31 people.

1871 – Joseph Gisbourne, a bricklayer's labourer, his wife Sarah and their 6 children live in one of the houses. By 1881, the family still live in the Yard, however their 3 eldest sons no longer live at home, but they now have 3 more daughters. By 1891 Joseph and Sarah still live in the Yard with only their 3 youngest daughters.

Also in 1891 one of the houses is occupied by John Colclough and his family. Another house is occupied by a Thomas Geraghty, originally from Ireland, and his family. By 1901 the two families still live in the Yard.

| Map Ref: 8 | Yard No. 97 | Long Street. 145-147 |

First known in 1768 – 2 houses and lived in continuously until 1937.

Date of demolition – after 1957 but from 1937 it was not inhabited but let as garages.

2 Residents were re-housed to Baddesley Ensor.

In a letter dated 13 February 1937, the solicitors Lester, Dixon & Jeffcoate instructed by the owner, Mr Frank Coleman, wrote regarding the Clearance Order made by the Council, relating to the 4 dwelling houses situated at Woolpack Yard on the grounds that these dwelling houses are capable of being used for garage purposes.

This yard had 5 houses with up to 24 people sharing a washhouse, and no privies.

Mr Coleman is willing to give an undertaking that the houses shall not be used for living accommodation after the Council have provided the tenants with suitable alternative accommodation.

This, it appears, was successful as the map for (Allen's Yard & Long Street No 4) Clearance Order 1956 shows Woolpack Yard being garages.

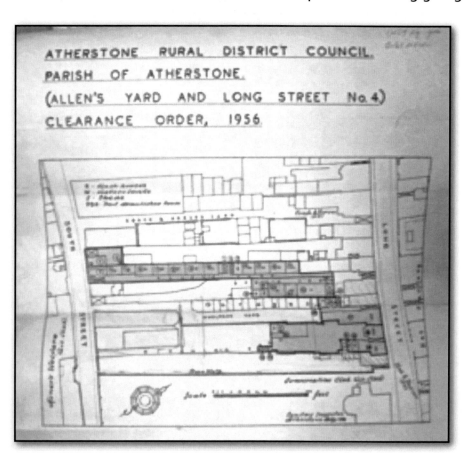

Frank Coleman not only owned houses in Atherstone he was also clerk to the Registrar of the Atherstone County Court. In an article in the Tamworth Herald dated 15 April 1911 it remarked that Mr Coleman had missed a sitting of the County Court due to ill health, the first time he had been absent for 34 years.

Frank was the son of a farmer from Grendon who moved with his family to the New Forest in Hampshire. On the death of his father, his mother, Sarah, became the head of the household with 336 acres of land in the New Forest and Frank was the youngest of 5 sons (1861 census). By 1871 he and his mother and one brother are back in Atherstone living in Railway Terrace. At age 32 in 1891 he is unmarried and still in Railway Terrace with his mother but by 1901 he is a widower with 2 small children living in South Street.

His position as Clerk to the Court must have paid quite well because on Tuesday, December 5th 1944, at an auction in the Red Lion, properties belonging to Frank Coleman were offered for sale, probably on his death at the age of about 85.

"Commodious dwelling house with possessions: 42 houses,17 garages etc. with a gross annual rent roll of £1,220 19s 4d including houses in Long Street, North Street, Cotton Mill Yard, Woolpack Yard and Allens Row."

WRIGHTS YARD

| Map Ref: 5 | Yard No. 77 | Long Street 204-206 |

Probably built before 1841 but only recorded in 2 censuses.

1841 and 1861.

The Maps

Guide to using the maps

Each yard has been given a number and then identified numerically along Long Street starting on the North Western end of Long Street between The White Hart Inn and the Queen Elizabeth School. Included within this area are the yards in Church Street and the one yard in North Street. The numbering then continues from the Eastern end of Long Street towards the Railway Station. On this side of the road some yards have also been identified in South Street, Station Street, Coleshill Road.

To find the location of a yard firstly consult the alphabetical list of yards and map numbers.

When the yard has been found note the map number and the yard number.

Then turn to the map required and find the yard number.

The line from the yard number will lead to the position of the yard. On the facing page the present day map will indicate where the yard was in relation to the buildings on Long Street today.

Yards by numbers and maps

Yard No	Map Number	Yard Name	Long Street No.	
1	1	White Hart Yard	White Hart	
2	1	Ortons Court/Yard	8-10	See Meads Yard (3)
3	1	Meads Yard	8-10	Also known as Ortons Yard (2)
4	1	Rumseys Yard	10-12	
5	1	Garden Row	14-16	
6	1	Cleoburys Yard	16-18	Also known as Windridges Yard (7)
7	1	Windridges Yard	16-18	See Cleoburys Yard (6)
8	1	Throwers Yard	20-22	
9	1	Lagoes Court/Buildings	20-26	
10	1	Ram Yard	28-30	Also known as Whites Yard (11)
11	1	Whites Court	28-30	See Ram Yard (10)
12	1	White Bear Yard	30-32	Also known as Friars Yard (13)
13	1	Friars Yard	30-32	See White Bear Yard (12)
14	1	Roes Yard	34-36	See Rogers Buildings (16)
15	1	Mustons Yard	34-36	See Rogers Buildings (16)
16	1	Rogers Buildings/Yards	34-36	Also known as Roes Yard (14) Mustons Yard (15)
17	1	Crown Yard	44-46	
18	2	Jeffcotts Yard	46-48	See Brown Bear Yard (19)
19	2	Brown Bear Yard	46-48	Also known as Jeffcotts Yard (18)
20	2	Hollybush Yard	62-64	See Blowers Yard (21)
21	2	Blowers Yard	62-64	Also known as Hollybush Yard (20)
22	2	Fords Yard/Buildings	64-66	Also known as Wimburys Buildings (23)
23	2	Wimburys Buildings	64-66	See Fords Yard (22)
24	2	Phoenix Yard	Church St	Also known as Simmonds Yard (25)
25	2	Simmonds Yard	Church St	See Phoenix Yard (24)
26	2	Angel Yard	Church St	
27	2	Ormes Yard	Church St	
28	3	Swan Yard	North St	
29	3	Millers Yard	94-96	
30	3	Mustons Yard	100-102	See Pinchbacks Yard (31)
31	3	Pinchbacks Yard	100-102	Also known as Mustons Yard (30)
32	3	Vinraces Row	118-120	
33	3	Whitbys Yard	122-124	
34	4	Westons Yard	124-126	See Brooks Yard (36)
35	4	Hoggs Yard	124-126	See Brooks Yard (36)

36	4	Brooks Yard	124-126	Also known as Hoggs Yard (35) and Westons Yard (34)
37	4	Hat and Beaver Yard	128-130	
38	4	Ellis Yard	134-136	See Old Plough Yard (40)
39	4	Wrights Yard	134-136	See Old Plough Yard (40)
40	4	Old Plough Yard	134-136	Also known as Wrights Yard (39) Ellis Yard (38)
41	4	Millers Yard	136-138	See Bakers Yard (42)
42	4	Bakers Yard	136-138	Also known as Millers Yard (41) Bakers Yard (42) Veros Yard (43) Taylors Yard (44)
43	4	Veros Yard	136-138	See Bakers Yard (42)
44	4	Taylors Yard	136-138	See Bakers Yard (42)
45	4	Lawtons Yard	136-138	See Bakers Yard (42)
46	4	Hattons Yard	142-144	See Hudsons Yard (47)
47	4	Hudsons Yard	142-144	Also known as Hattons Yard (46)
48	4	Rowleys Yard	146-148	See Cross Keys Yard (49)
49	4	Cross Keys Yard	146-148	Also known as Rowleys Yard (48)
50	4	Mays Yard	150-152	
51	4	Black Horse Yard	156-158	
52	4	Smiths Yard	160-162	See Paynes Yard (53)
53	4	Paynes Yard	160-162	Also known as Smiths Yard (52)
54	4	Dolphin Yard	162-164	
55	4	Cotton Mill Yard	164-166	Also known as Coles Yard (56)
56	4	Coles Yard	164-166	See Cotton Mill Yard (55)
57	5	Friends Meeting House	172-174	
58	5	Kendricks Yard	176-178	See Congreves Yard (62)
59	5	Silks Court	176-178	See Congreves Yard (62)
60	5	Windridges Yard	176-178	See Congreves Yard (62)
61	5	Quimbys Yard	176-178	See Congreves Yard (62)
62	5	Congreves Yard	176-178	Also known as Kendricks Yard (58) Silks Court (59) Windridges Yard (60) Quimby Yard (61)
63	5	Gothards Row/Yard	178-180	See Mount Pleasant Yard (64)
64	5	Mount Pleasant	178-180	Also known as Gothards Row (63)
65	5	Mills Yard	186-188	
66	5	Ortons Yard	196-198	See Pittams Yard (67)
67	5	Pittams Yard	196-198	Also known as Ortons Yard (66) Copes Buildings (68)
68	5	Copes Yard/Buildings	196-198	See Pittams Yard (67)
69	5	Vinraces Yard	200-202	See Pearmans Yard (70)

70	5	Pearmans Yard	200-202	Also known as Vinraces Yard (69) Millers Yard (71)
71	5	Millers Yard	200-202	See Pearmans Yard (70)
72	5	Farmers Yard	202-204	See Mercers Buildings (74)
73	5	Paynes Buildings	202-204	See Mercers Buildings (74)
74	5	Mercers Buildings	202-204	Also known as Farmers Yard (72) Paynes Yard (73) Barsbys Yard (76)
75	5	Stantons Buildings	202-204	
76	5	Barsbys Yard	202-204	See Mercers Buildings (74)
77	5	Wrights Yard	204-206	
78	6	Paynes Lodging House	189-191	
79	7	Whites Yard	181-183	See Heatles Yard (80)
80	7	Heatles Buildings	181-183	Also known as Whites Yard (79)
81	7	Potters Yard	179-181	See Gisbournes Yard (82)
82	7	Gisbournes Yard	179-181	Also known as Potters Yard (81) Lucas Yard (83)
83	7	Lucas Yard	179-181	See Gisbournes Yard (82)
84	7	Baxters Buildings/ Knob Hill	South St	
85	7	Hallams Yard/Sq	171-173	
86	7	Corbetts Yard	167-169	See Simonds Yard (89)
87	7	Hulls Yard	167-169	See Simonds Yard (89)
88	7	Haddons Yard	167-169	See Simonds Yard (89)
89	7	Simonds Yard / Buildings	167-169	Also known as Corbetts Yard (86) Hulls Yard (87) Haddons Yard (88)
90	7	Mousleys Yard	167-169	See Sales Yard (92)
91	7	Biddles Yard	167-169	See Sales Yard (92)
92	7	Sales Yard / Buildings	167-169	Also known as Mousleys Yard (90) Biddles Yard (91)
93	7	Kent Yard	163-165	See Radford Buildings (108)
94	7	Radfords Buildings/ Yard	163-165	Also knoan as Kent Yard(93)
95	7	Gains Yard	149-151	See Kitchins Yard (96)
96	7	Kitchens Yard / Buildings	149-151	Also known as Gains Yard (95)
97	8	Woolpack Yard	145-147	
98	8	Bonds Yard	141-143	Also known as Briggs Yard (99)
99	8	Briggs Yard	141-143	See Bonds Yard (98)
100	8	Allens Yard	141-143	
101	8	Coach & Horses Yard	135-137	
102	8	Bournes Yard	131-133	

103	8	Old House Yard	127-129	
104	8	Hincks Yard	123-125	
105	8	Gees Yard	113-115	See Hattons Yard (106)
106	8	Hattons Yard	113-115	Also known as Gees Yard (105)
107	8	Everetts Yard	109-111	See Radford Buildings (108)
108	8	Radford Yard	109-111	Also known as Everetts Yard (107)
109	8	Bassetts Yard	109-111	See Stevensons Yard (112)
110	8	Sands Yard	109-111	See Stevensons Yard (112)
111	8	Hambreys Yard	109-111	See Stevensons Yard (112)
112	8	Stevensons Yard	109-111	Also known as Bassetts Yard (109) Sands Yard (110) Hambreys Yard (111)
113	8	Winters Yard/ Terrace	103-105	
114	11	Richmond Hill Yard	Coleshill Rd	
115	11	Fox Yard	Coleshill Rd	
116	11	Haddons Yard	Station St	
117	11	White Lion Yard	Station St	
118	11	Clarks Yard	Station St	
119	11	Innage Terrace	Station St	
120	9	Black Boy Yard	91-93	
121	9	Blue Bell Yard	87-89	
122	9	Gutteridge Yard	83-85	See Woods Yard (124)
123	9	Ashers Yard	83-85	See Woods Yard (124)
124	9	Woods Yard	83-85	Also known as Gutteridges Yard (122) Ashers Yard (123)
125	9	Hand & Bottle Yard	81-83	
126	9	Nelson Yard	75-77	
127	9	Kings Arms Yard	73-75	
128	9	T Veros Yard		
129	9	Druids Arms Yard	67-69	Also known as Marriotts Yard (130)
130	9	Marriotts Yard	67-69	See Druids Arms Yard (129)
131	9	Partridges Yard	67-69	See Spencers Yard (133)
132	9	Barnes Yard	67-69	See Spencers Yard (133)
133	9	Spencers Yard/ Buildings	67-69	Also known as Partridges Yard (131) Barnes Yard (132) Lloyds Yard (134)
134	9	Lloyds Yard	67-69	See Spencers Yard (133)
135	9	Handford Yard	63-65	See Factoty Yard (136)
136	9	Factory Yard	63-65	Also known as Handford Yard (135)
137	9	Co-op Yard	59-61	
138	9	Rogers Yard	49-51	See Swan and Two Necks Yard (139)
139	9	Swan and Two Necks Yard	49-51	Also known as Rogers Yard (138)

140	10	Roes Yard	Station St	
141	10	Wildays Yard	37-39	Also known as Binghams Yard (142)
142	10	Binghams Row	37-39	See Willdays Yard (141)
143	10	Cordingleys Yard	33-35	Also known as Collins Yard (144) Pearmans Yard (145) Whites Yard (146) Woodroffes Row (147)
144	10	Collins Yard	33-35	See Cordingleys Yard (143)
145	10	Pearmans Yard	33-35	See Cordingleys Yard (143)
146	10	Whites Yard	33-35	See Cordingleys Yard (143)
147	10	Woodruffes Row	33-35	See Cordingleys Yard (143)
148	10	Woodman Yard	Station St	
149	10	Wheatsheaf Yard	29-31	
150	10	Veros Yard/Terrace	25-27	Also known as Roadknights Yard (151)
151	10	Road Knights Yard	25-27	See Veros Yard (150)
152	10	Baker Terrace	Station St	Also known as Simonds Yard (153) Nurthalls Yard (154)
153	10	Simonds Yard	Station St	See Bakers Terrace (152)
154	10	Nurthalls Yard	Station St	See Bakers Terrace (152)
155	10	Johnsons Buildings	17-19 Dem	Also known as Earps Yard (156)
156	10	Earps Yard	17-19 Dem	See Johnsons Buildings (155)
157	10	Spencers Yard	17-19 Dem	See Johnsons Buildings (155)
158	10	Avins Yard	23-25	
159	10	Boss Yard	19-21	
160	10	Old House Yard 2	13-15 Dem	
161	10	Veros Yard	9-11 Dem	
162	10	Tates Yard	Station St Dem	
163	10	Railway Tavern Yard	Demolished	
164	10	Wash Pad Yard	Station St Dem	

The Maps

**Old archive maps (approx. 1888)
and
Present Day maps (2004)
indicating the position
of each Yard**

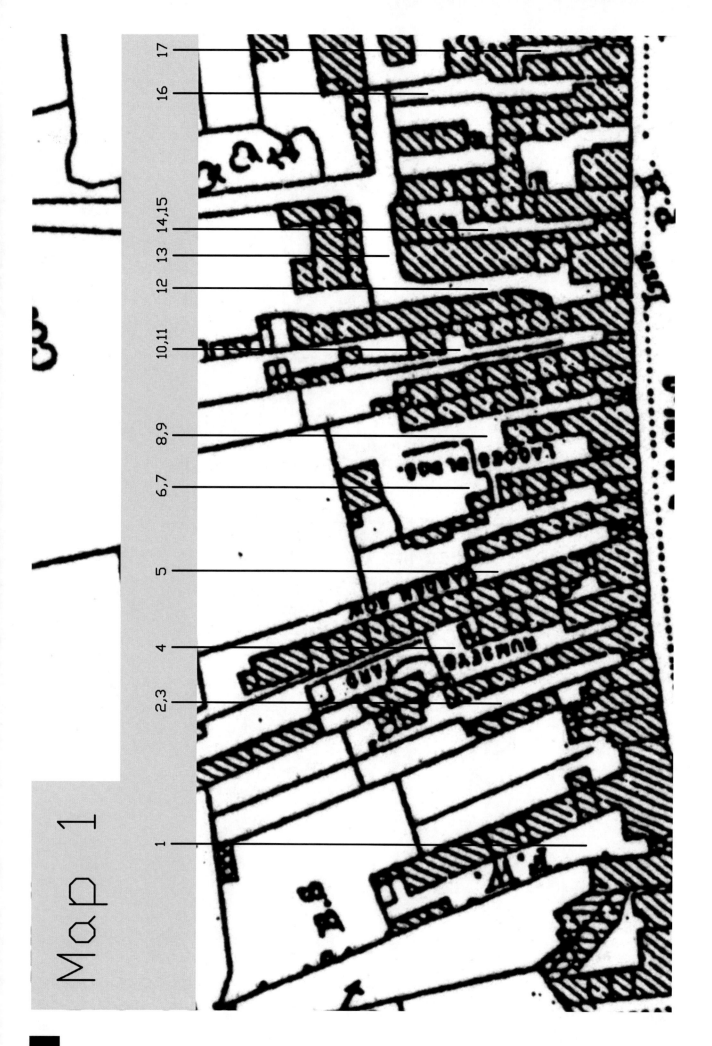

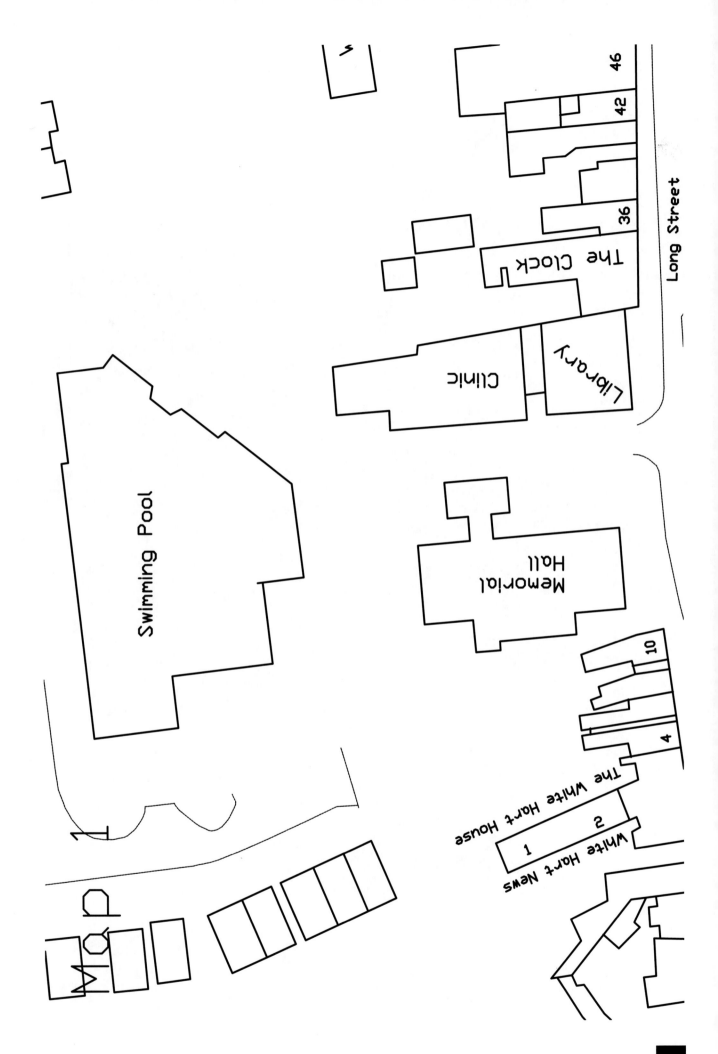

Long Street

46

42

36

The Clock

Clinic

Library

Swimming Pool

Memorial
Hall

10

4

The White Hart House

White Hart News

1

2

M a p

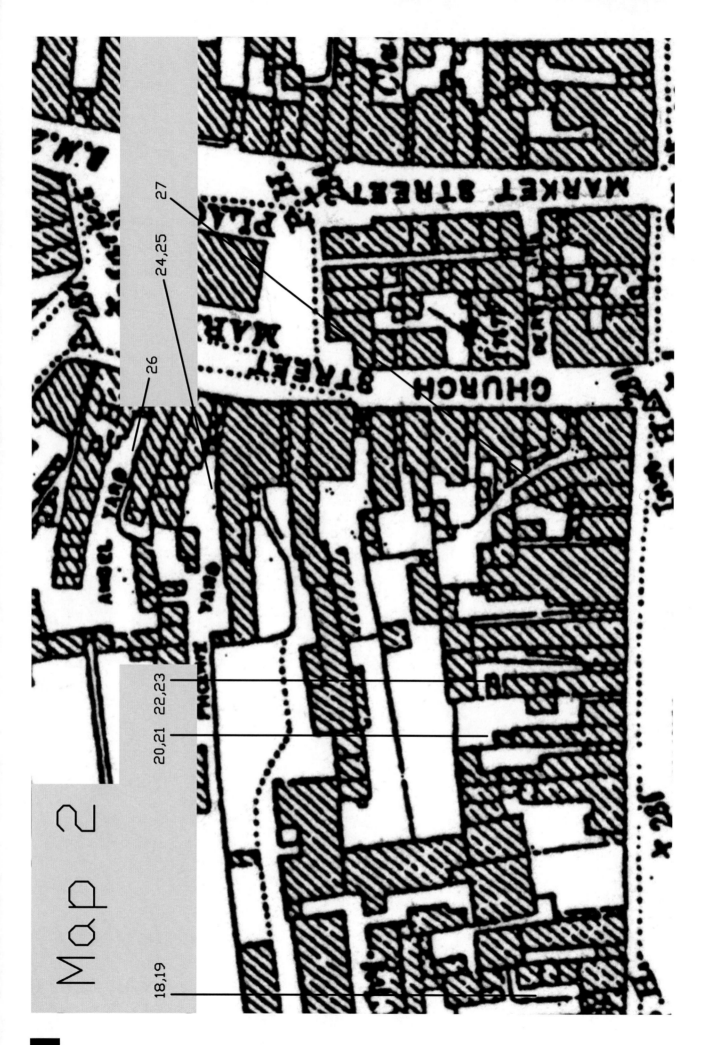

Map 2

18,19

20,21 22,23

26

24,25

27

MARKET STREET

CHURCH STREET

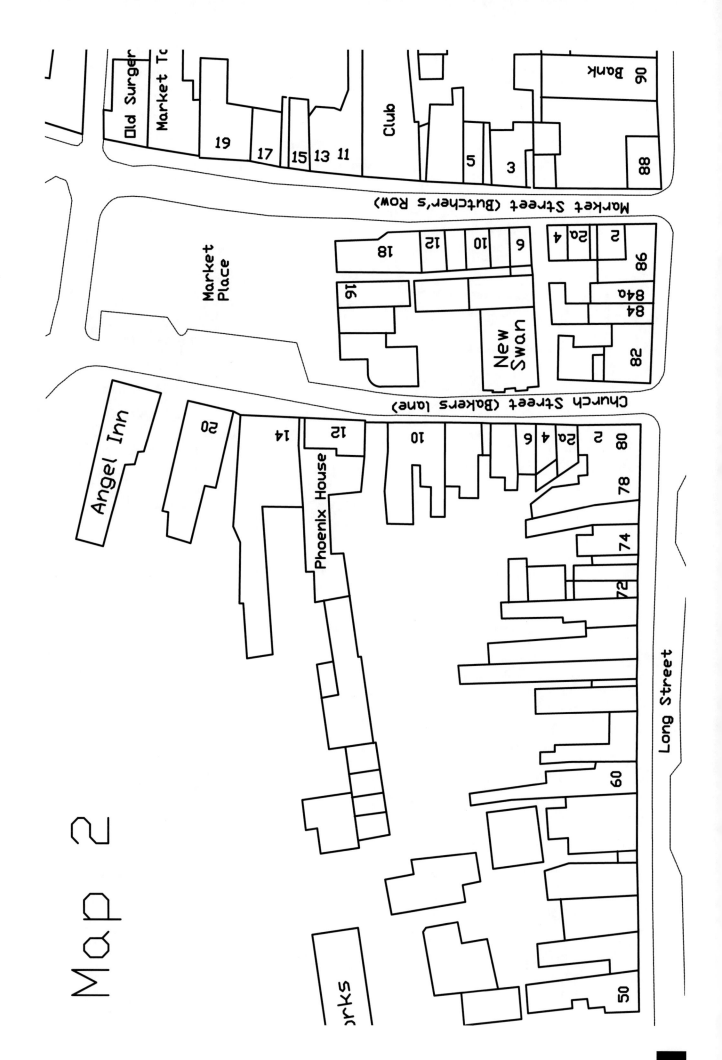

Map 2

Old Surger...
Market T...

19
17 15 13 11

Club

5

3

Bank
90

88

Market Street (Butcher's Row)

Market Place

16   18
        12
        10
        6

4 2a
      2

98
84a 84

82

28

New Swan

Church Street (Bakers lane)

Angel Inn

20

14

Phoenix House

12

10

6 4 2a
        2
80
78

74

72

...rks

69

60

50

Long Street

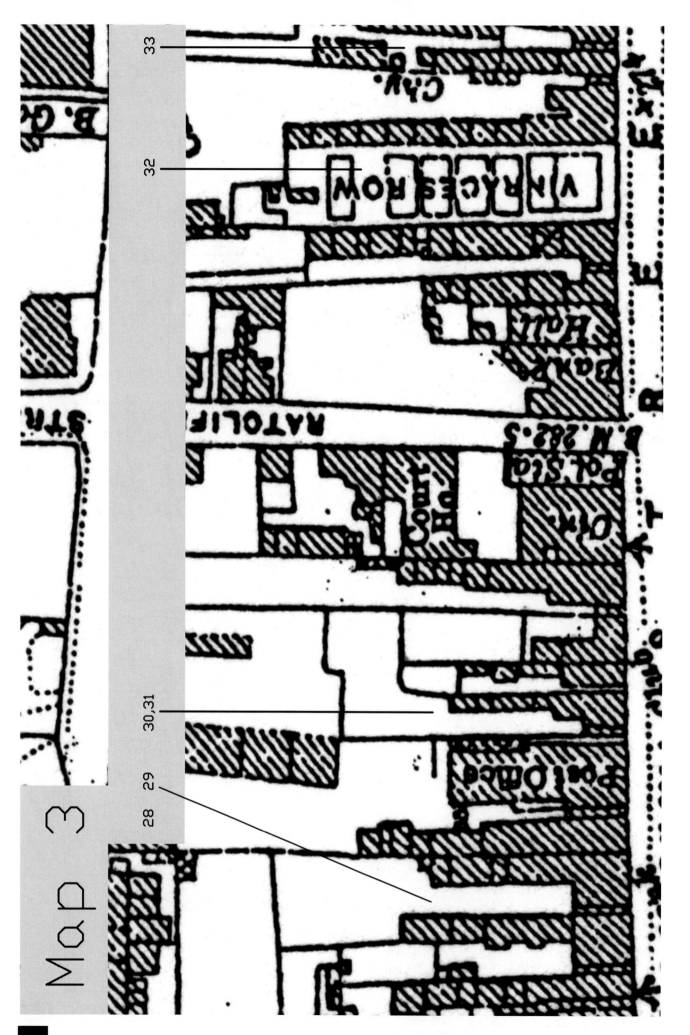

Map 3

33

32

30,31

29

28

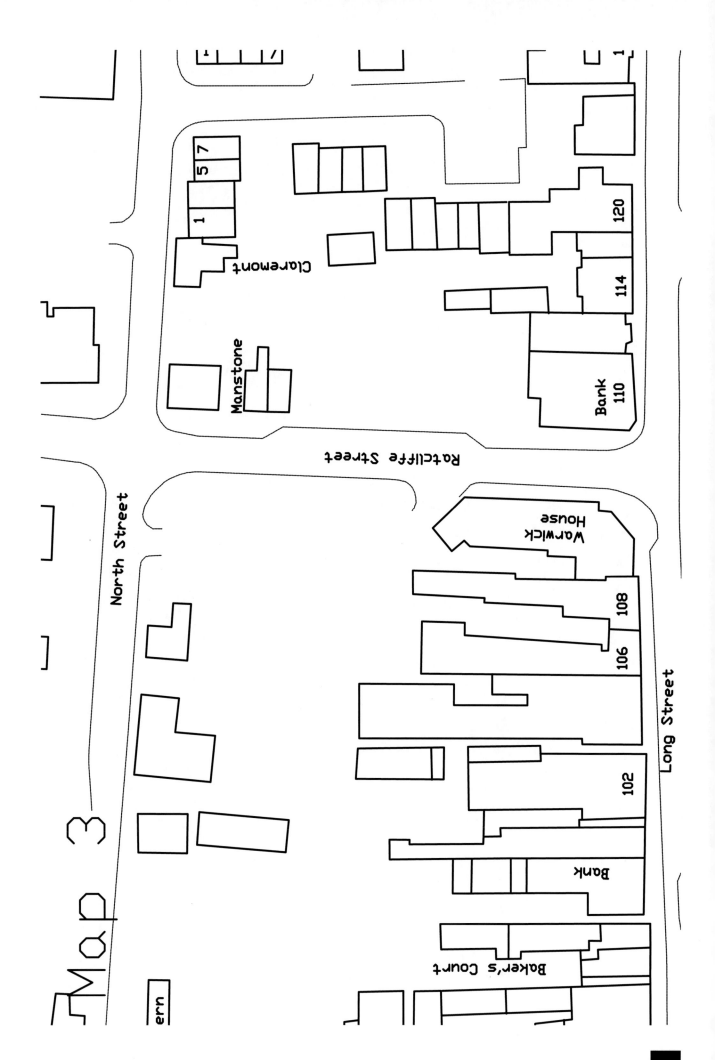

Map 3

North Street

Ratcliffe Street

Long Street

Claremont

Manstone

1

5 7

120

114

Bank 110

Warwick House

108

106

102

Bank

Baker's Court

ern

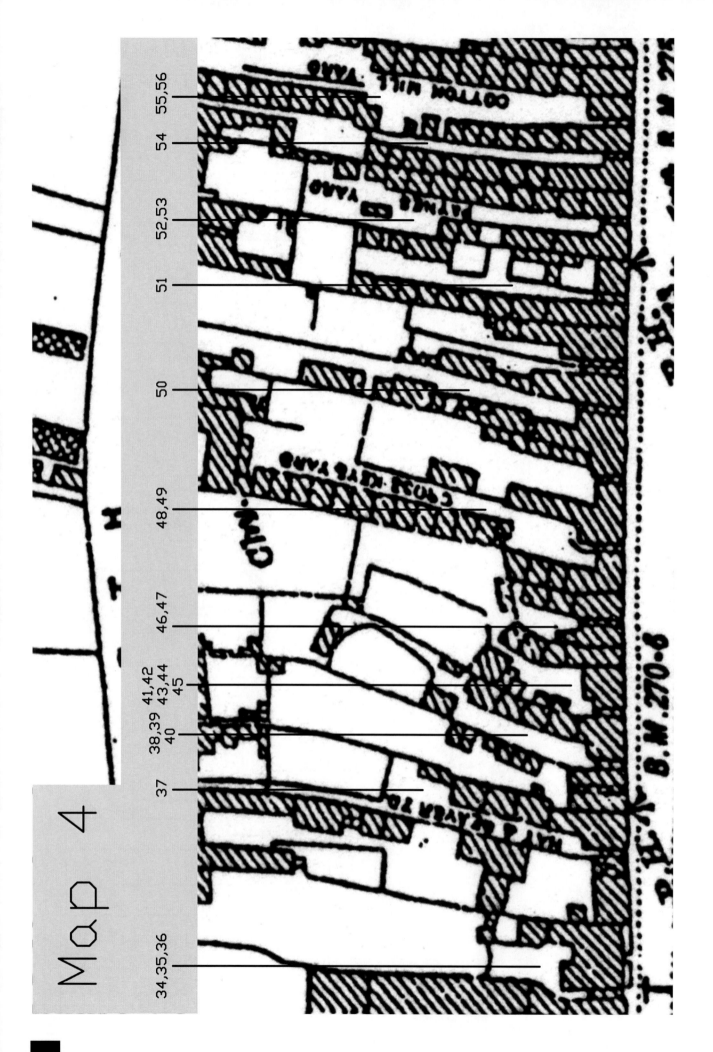

Map 4

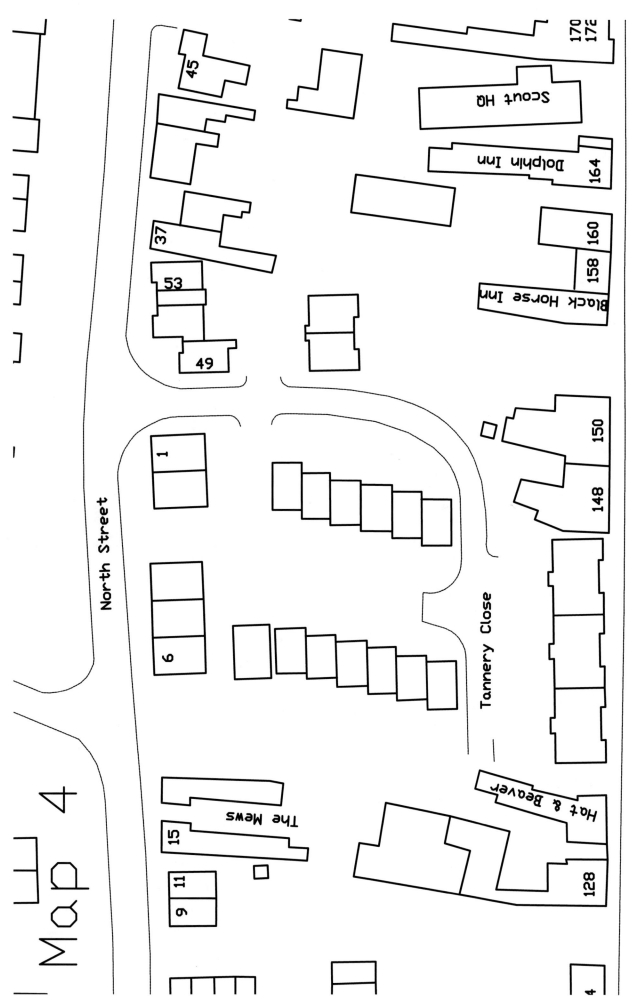

Map 4

North Street

The Mews

Tannery Close

Long Street

45

37

53

49

1

6

15

9 11

9

Scout HQ

Dolphin Inn

164

158 160

Black Horse Inn

150

148

128

Hat & Beaver

170
172

4

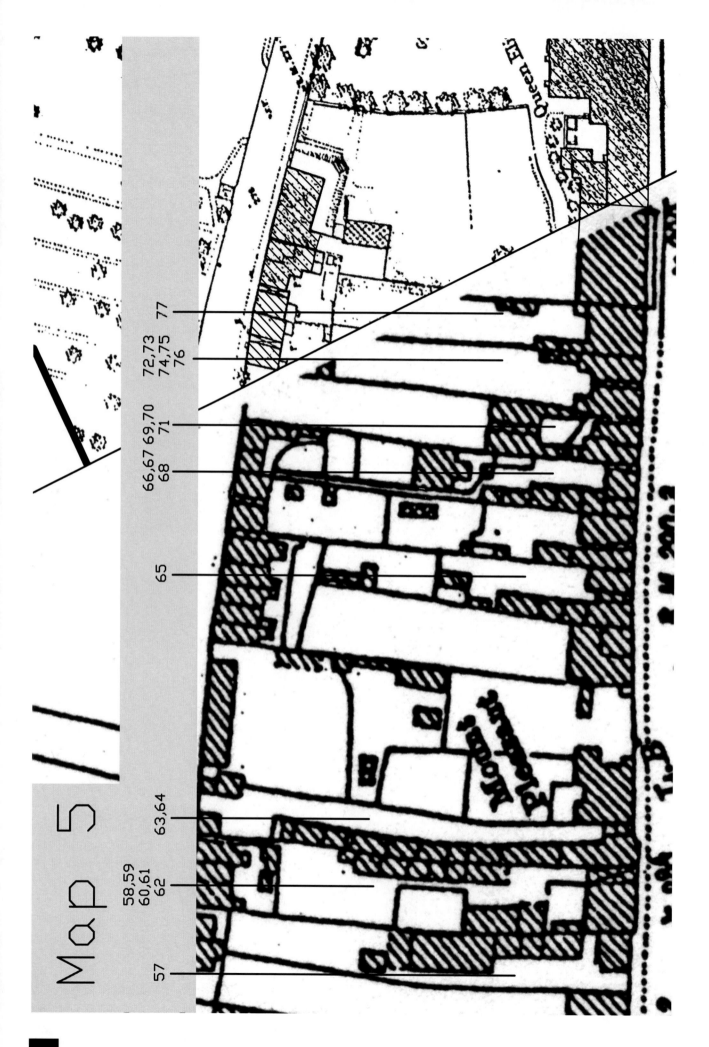

Map 5

58,59
60,61
62

63,64

57

65

66,67 69,70
68   71

72,73
74,75
76

77

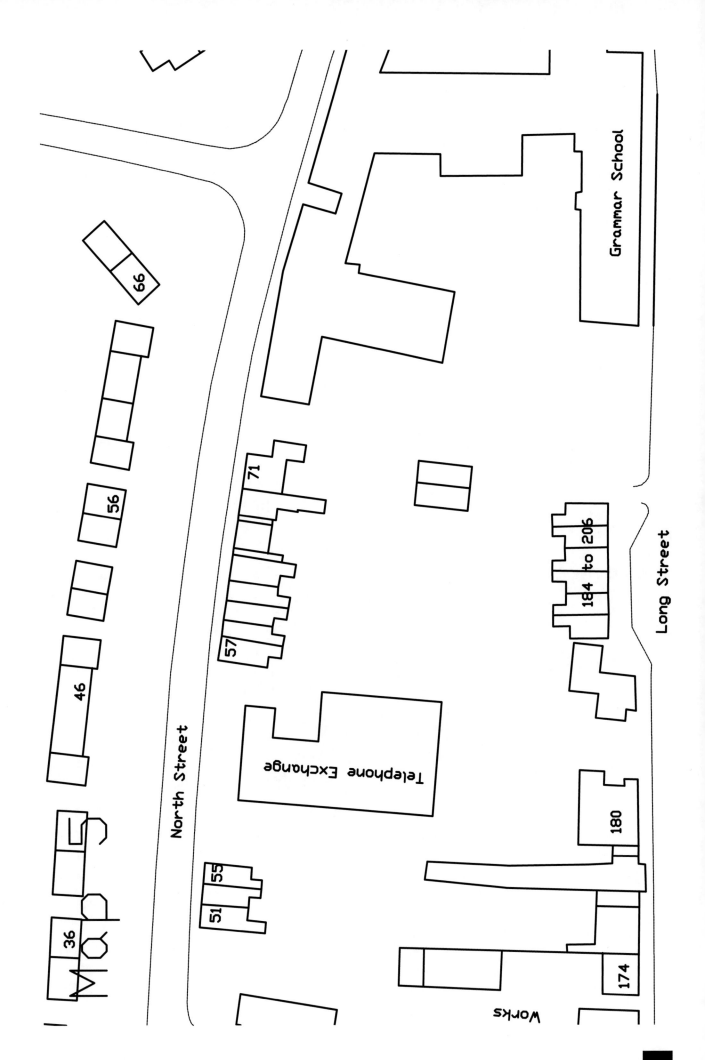

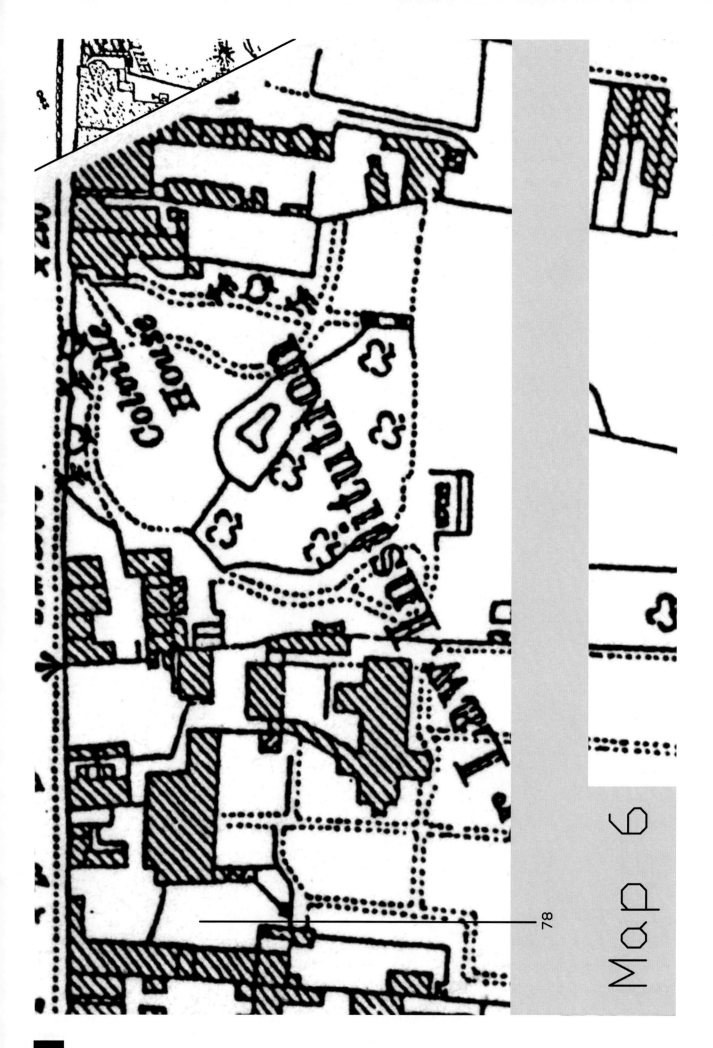

Map 6

78

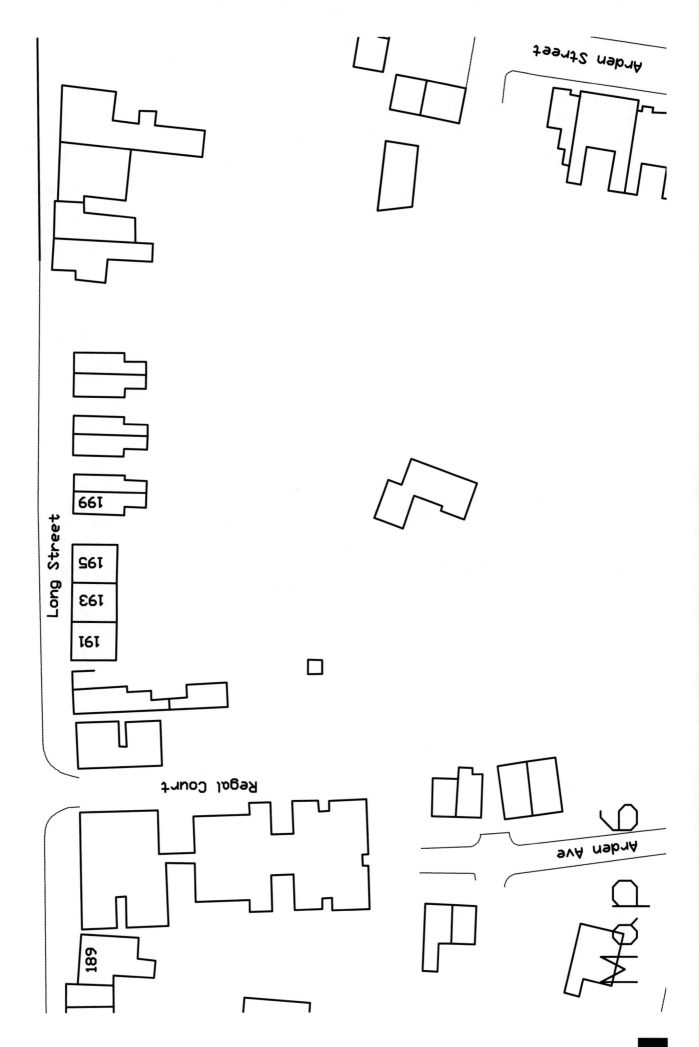

Arden Street

Long Street

199

195

193

191

Regal Court

181

Arden Ave

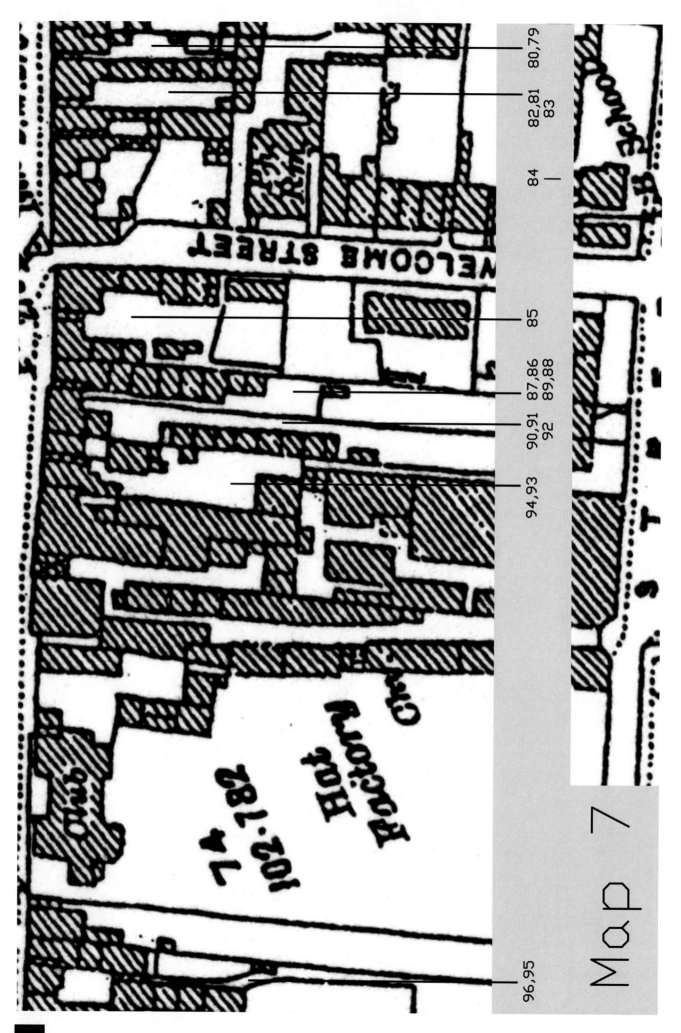

Map 7

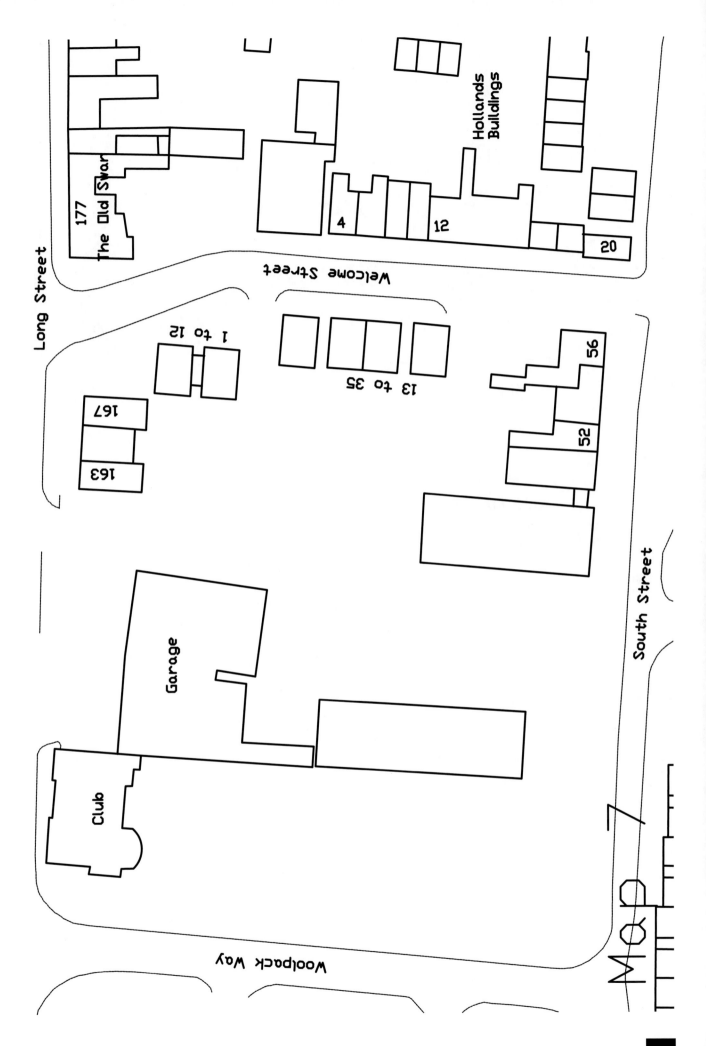

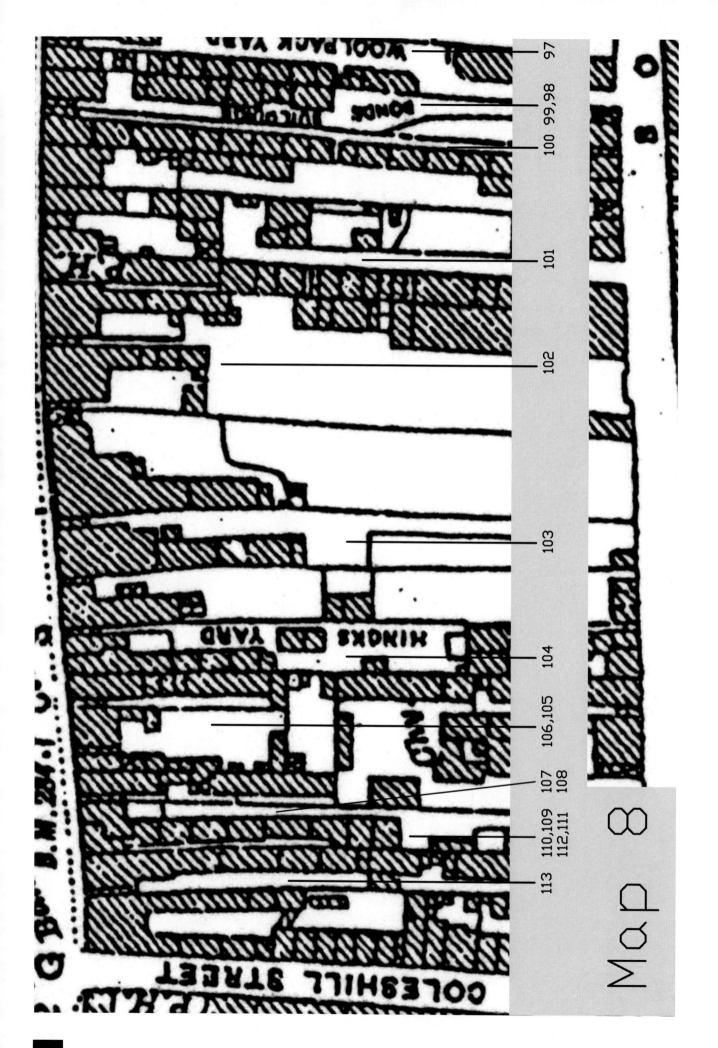

Map 8

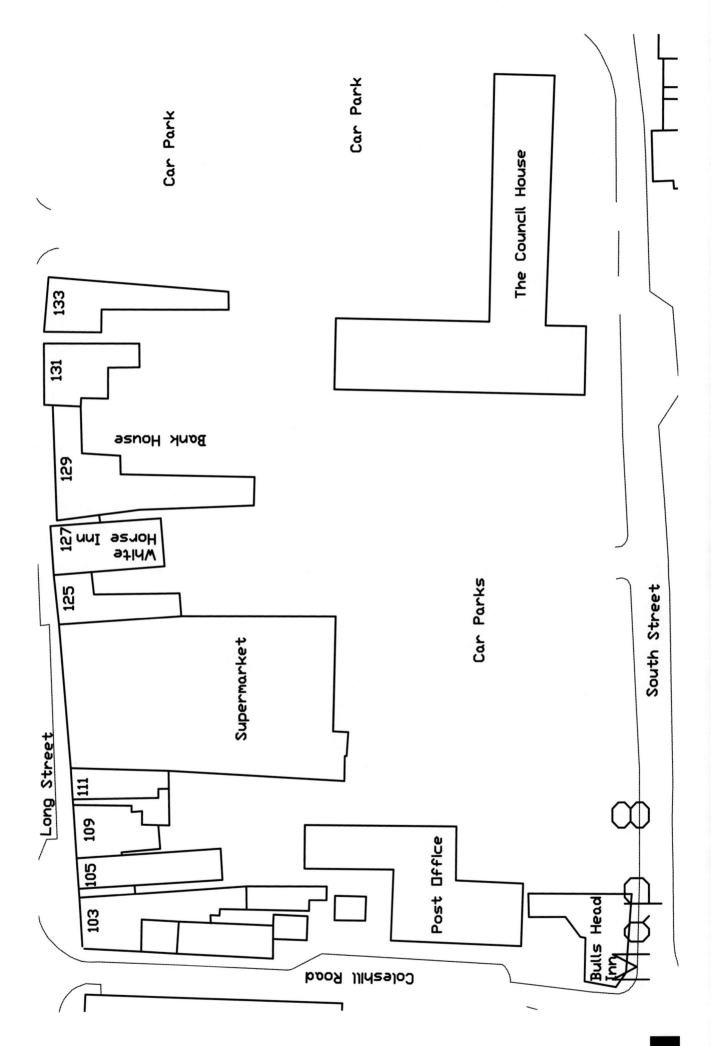

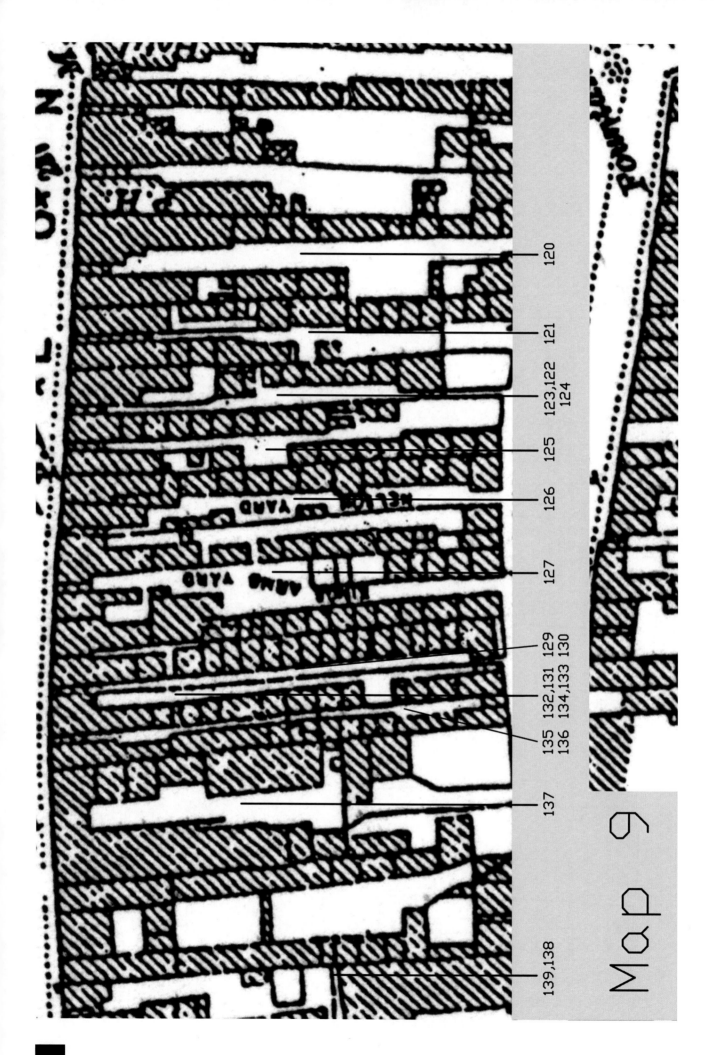

Map 9

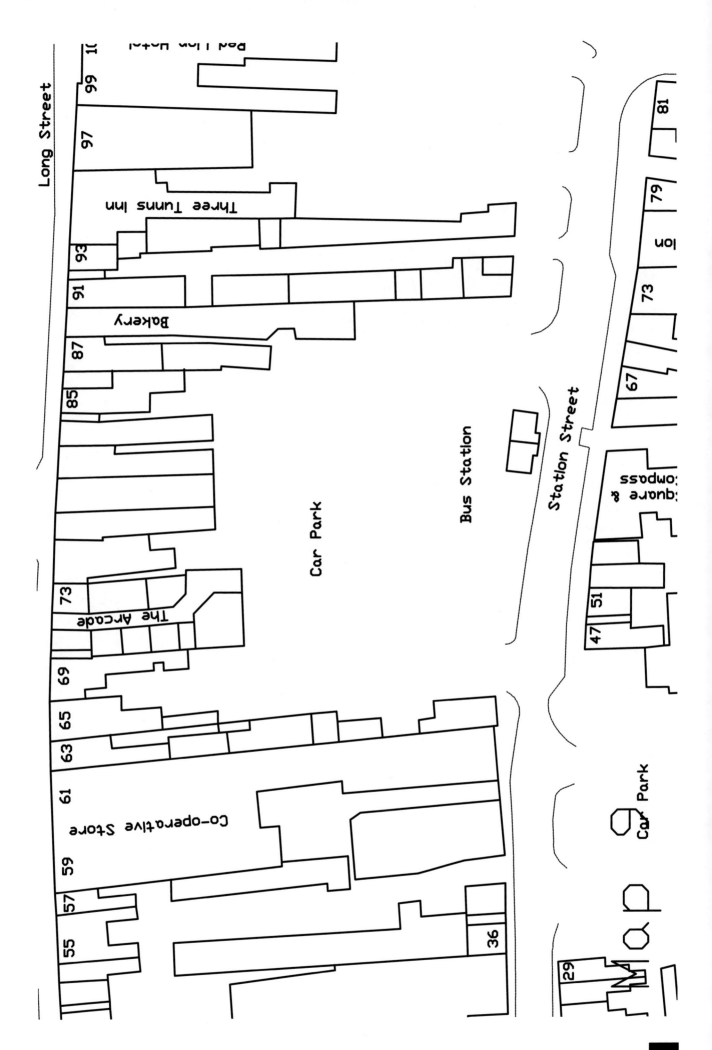

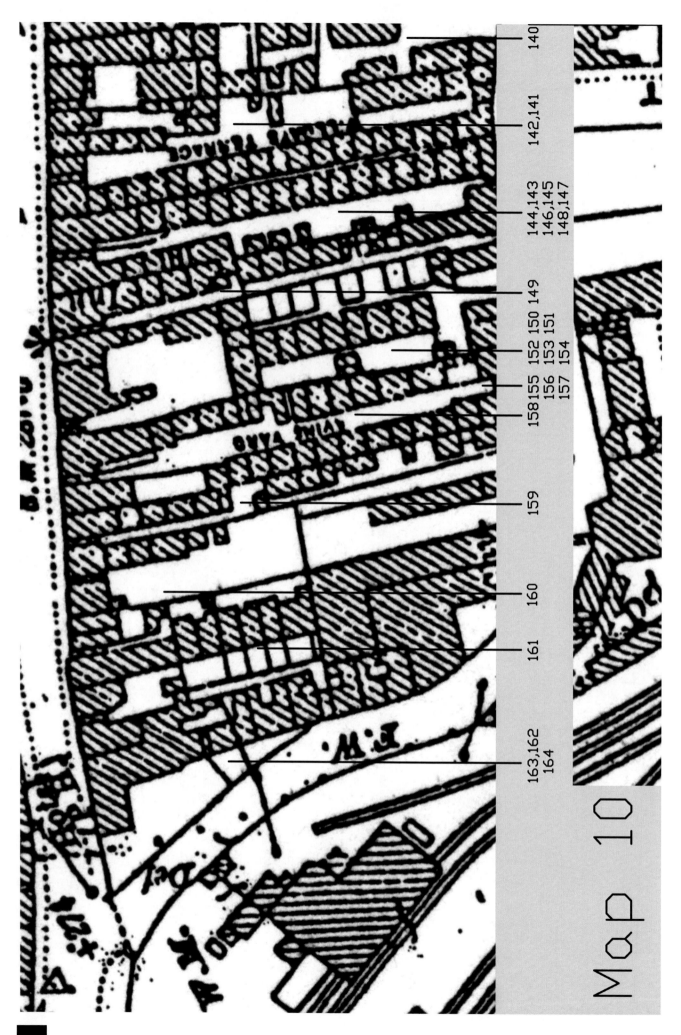

140

142,141

144,143
146,145
148,147

149
152 150
153 151
154

158 155
156
157

159

160

161

163,162
164

Map 10

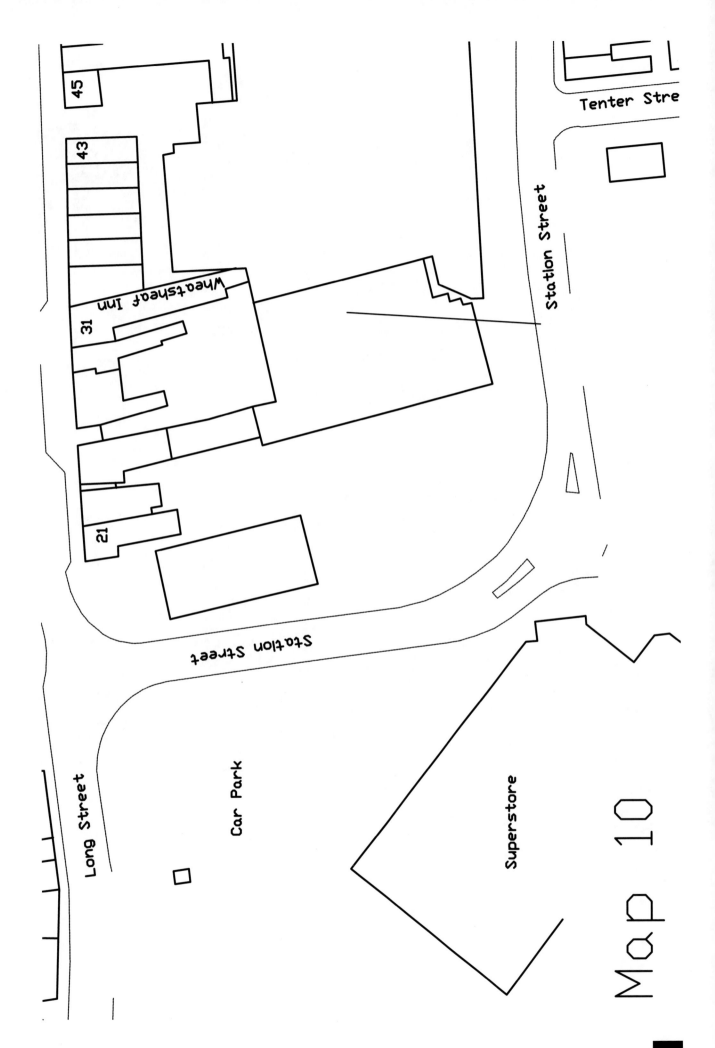

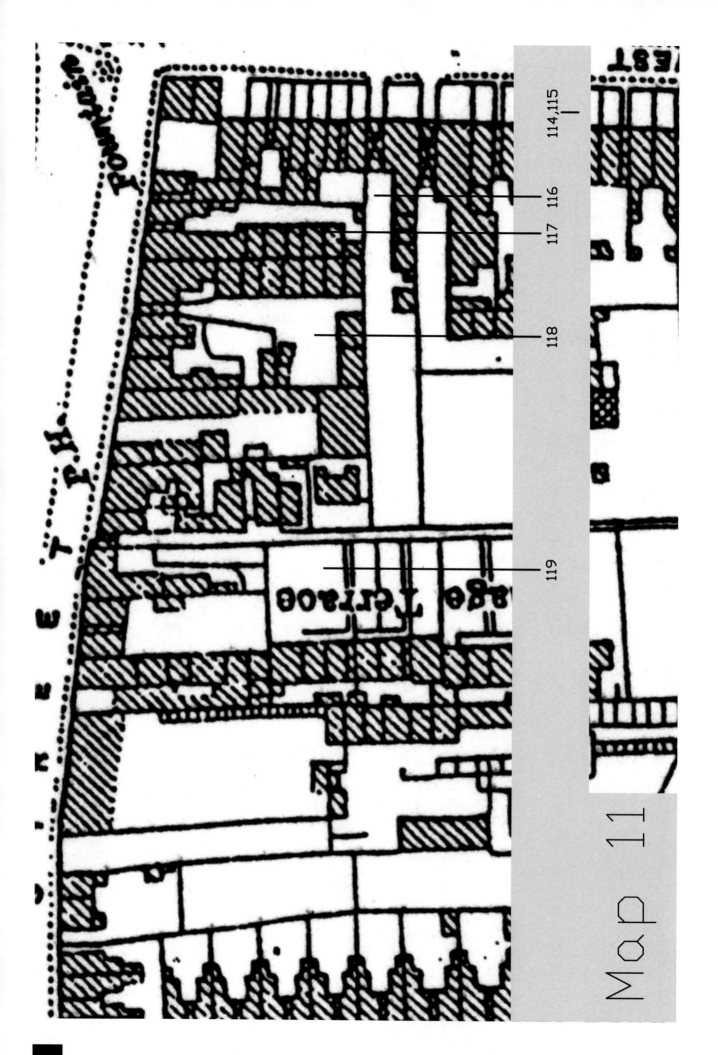

114,115

116

117

118

119

Map 11

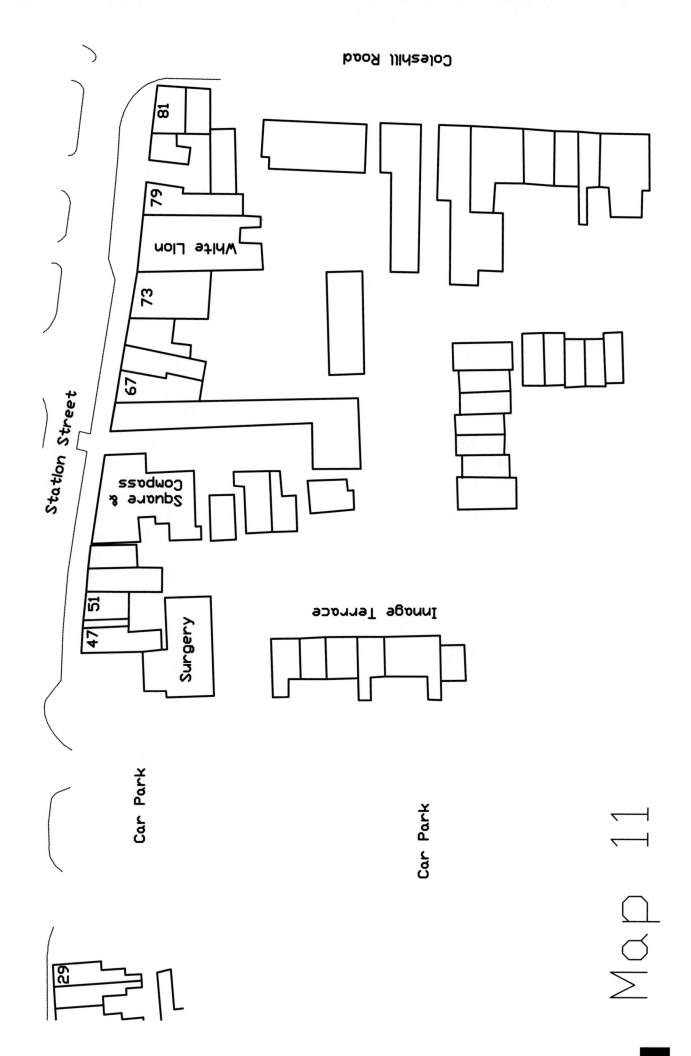

Coleshill Road

Station Street

81

79

White Lion

73

67

Square & Compass

Surgery

51

47

29

Innage Terrace

Car Park

Car Park

Map 11

Appendix A
Herring Report 1911

Dr. John Herring came to Atherstone in 1880 to practise medicine with his partner Dr. Robert Mears. They had a surgery in the Market Place and in addition Dr. Herring served as Medical Officer of Health to the Atherstone Rural District Council. Part of his contract was to write an annual report to the council. His reports became increasingly critical of conditions in the yards, with his report for 1911 being so damning that it was taken up by Warwickshire County Council and questions were asked in Parliament.

Written a few months after the Census of 1911 Dr. Herring was able to be very accurate in his statistics pointing out that, taking into account the fact that the population of Atherstone had increased only slightly since the last Census, deaths from TB and infectious diseases were the highest ever recorded and infant deaths were 50% up on the previous year's figures. 15 infants had died within hours of birth despite Government legislation in 1902 and 1907 designed to avoid such tragedies.

1902 Midwives Act: This act made it law that all midwives should be trained and registered. A Central Midwives Board was formed to set the standards that midwives would have to work to.

1907 Notification of Births Act: this act stated that the local Medical Officer of Health had to be informed as soon as possible after a child had been born. It was then his job to arrange for a trained health visitor to call on the mother at her home and teach her how to protect the baby' health.

He reports that a Scarlet Fever epidemic had been raging for more than three years due to the impossibility of isolating new cases. A new fever hospital at Grendon was not yet ready for use but when it was it would have hot and cold water, a laundry and proper sewage treatment. The daughter of the vicar of Grendon, Elizabeth Crawley-Boevey remembers very well being admitted with her sisters to the newly opened Grendon Fever Hospital when they contracted Scarlet Fever.

Grendon Fever Hospital in the late 20th century when the building was used as a boarding kennels.

He comments on the inadequate water supply to the town resulting in the supply being cut off at night to save stocks; this is echoed in comments by the Clerk to Atherstone Town Council.

The bulk of Herring's report details his findings as Superintendant charged with carrying out the requirements of 'The Town Planning Act of 1909'. As he says "it would be difficult to find a locality in which the Housing Act is more needed." He names 60 yards with an average of 4.43 people in each house, with 30 houses containing 9 or more people in each of them.

The *DISABILITIES* as he calls them are lack of hygiene, stagnant and impure air, narrow entrances, inaccessible to carts, through which everything has to be carried including the sick and corpses. He describes one yard in which contractors have to make 20 or 25 journeys wheeling tubs of filth past the open doors of 15 houses.

The body cart used by the undertakers to remove corpses from the yards

Because the yards had been constructed on private land they were not accessible to anyone other than residents so they were not swept by the council. He found not a single street lamp in any yard and the Police did not patrol them and could only enter if there was a disturbance.

As to the houses themselves, he found them small, lacking in any amenity such as piped water or drains. Everything had to be done in the crowded downstairs room so privacy was non-existent leading to a disheartened wife and a man, after a day's work, choosing to go out to the public house for brighter surroundings which lead to "intemperance and improvidence". In one yard Dr. Herring found a population density of 545 persons to the acre, compared to 160 persons to the acre in Birmingham's worst ward. During the year of his report he recorded 18 child deaths in the yards compared with 12 deaths in the open part of Atherstone despite there being double the population outside the yards.

The main recommendation of the report was to open up the yards by removing houses at each end so as to allow air to flow freely. He acknowledges that merely to knock down the worst of the houses would cause problems as there was a shortage of houses in the town, but the forced removal of some houses under the Housing Act would make a difference. He carries this idea of opening up the town on to Long Street where, had his ideas been carried out, there would have been a series of cross roads allowing health-giving breezes to blow north, south, east and west.

Despite this damning report only 59 houses were inspected during the year; seven were demolished while the rest were renovated by the landlords to bring them up to a habitable condition.

The statistics included in the report showed that the doctor's main concern in 1911 was the high incidence of infant deaths and preventable deaths from infectious diseases which spread like wildfire through the insanitary yards.

Appendix B
A typical Clearance Order

91,695.   (30*th August*, 1937.)

HOUSING ACT, 1936.

Order confirming clearance order.

RURAL DISTRICT OF ATHERSTONE.

WHEREAS the Council of the Rural District of Atherstone (in this order referred to as " the Council ") being the local authority for the said rural district for the purposes of Part I of the Housing Act, 1930 on the 1st day of December 1936 passed a resolution declaring the area thereby specified to be a clearance area within the meaning of section 1 of the said Act ;

AND WHEREAS on the 26th day of January 1937 in pursuance of their powers under section 26 of the Housing Act, 1936 the Council made an order (in this order referred to as " the clearance order ") for the demolition of the buildings in the said area being the buildings specified in the schedule to the clearance order and have submitted the clearance order to the Minister of Health (in this order referred to as " the Minister ") for confirmation ;

AND WHEREAS no objection to the clearance order has been made by any person upon whom notice thereof was served by the Council and the Minister has decided to confirm the clearance order :

NOW THEREFORE the Minister in pursuance of all powers enabling him in that behalf hereby confirms the clearance order in the form set out hereunder.

This order may be cited as the Atherstone Rural (Congrave's Buildings) Housing Confirmation Order 1937.

Order made by the Council for the demolition of buildings in a clearance area, as confirmed by the Minister of Health.

1. The buildings specified in the schedule hereto being the buildings which are delineated and shown coloured pink on the map shall be demolished.

SCHEDULE.

Reference numbers on map. 1.	Description and situation of the buildings. 2.	Owners or reputed owners. 3.	Lessees or reputed lessees. 4.	Occupiers (except tenants for a month or less period than a month). 5.	Period from the date when the order becomes operative within which the building is to be vacated. 6.
1	Dwelling-house, Congraves Buildings	Charles Taylor	—	—	Four months.
2	Dwelling-house, do.	do.	—	—	do.
3	Wash-house, do.	do.	—	—	do.
4	Ashpit, do.	do.	—	—	do.
5	Water Closet, do.	do.	—	—	do.

ATHERSTONE RURAL DISTRICT COUNCIL.
PARISH OF ATHERSTONE
(CONGRAVE'S BUILDINGS)
CLEARANCE ORDER 1937.
ATHERSTONE.

MINISTRY OF HEALTH

A 6.2.37
1390/123

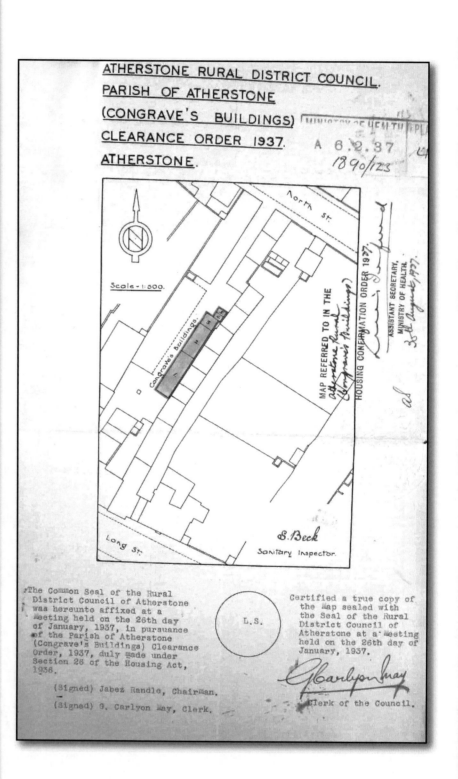

Scale - 1:500.

North St.

Congrave's Buildings

Long St.

MAP REFERRED TO IN THE
Atherstone Rural
(Congrave's Buildings)
HOUSING CONFIRMATION ORDER 1937.

ASSISTANT SECRETARY,
MINISTRY OF HEALTH.
30th August, 1937.

S. Beck
Sanitary Inspector.

The Common Seal of the Rural
District Council of Atherstone
was hereunto affixed at a
meeting held on the 26th day
of January, 1937, in pursuance
of the Parish of Atherstone
(Congrave's Buildings) Clearance
Order, 1937, duly made under
Section 26 of the Housing Act,
1936.

(Signed) Jabez Randle, Chairman.

(Signed) G. Carlyon May, Clerk.

L.S.

Certified a true copy of
the Map sealed with
the Seal of the Rural
District Council of
Atherstone at a meeting
held on the 26th day of
January, 1937.

Clerk of the Council.

Appendix C
A transcribed census page

1881 Census Form

Country: ENGLAND AND WALES   Piece #: RG11/ 3058   Folio: 55
Page: 2D   Enumeration Date:

The undermentioned Houses are situate within the Boundaries of the

Civil Parish [or Township] of: ATHERSTONE
Rural Sanitary District of: ATHERSTONE
Ecclesiastical Parish or District of: ST MARY ATHERSTONE

No. of Schedule	ROAD, STREET, etc. and No. or NAME of HOUSE	HOUSES Inhabited	HOUSES Uninhabited (U) or Building (B)	NAME and Surname of each Person	RELATION to Head of Family	Condition as to Marriage	AGE Males	AGE Females	Rank, profession or OCCUPATION	WHERE BORN	If (1) Deaf & Dumb (2) Blind (3) Imbecile or Idiot (4) Lunatic
95	HINCKS YD	1		EDWARD CLIPPERTON	HEAD	MAR	22		LABOURER	WARWICK ATHERSTONE	
				EMMA do	WIFE	do		22		LEICESTER	
96				CLARA ORTON	LODGER	do		21	HAT TRIMMER	WARWICK GRENDON	
97	HINCKS YARD	1		JAMES HART	HEAD	MAR	43		LABOURER BRICKLAYER	WARWICK ATHERSTONE	
				MARY do	WIFE	do		50		TAMWORTH	
				EDWARD WALL	STEPSON	UNM	22		BRAZIER	GRENDON	
				JOHN WALL	do do	do	15		HATTER	ATHERSTONE	
98	HINCKS YARD	1		JAMES PAYNE	HEAD	MAR	36		BODY MAKER (HATTER)	GRENDON	
				JANE do	WIFE	do		30	HAT TRIMMER	ATHERSTONE	
				CHARLES do	SON	UNM	3			do	
99	HINCKS YD	1		JOHN MILLERSHIPS	HEAD	MAR	26		COAL MINER	do COVENTRY	
				SARAH do	WIFE	do		38	HAT TRIMMER	do ATHERSTONE	
				HENRIETTA do	DAU	UNM		9		do	
				ROLAND do	SON	do	5			do	
				JOSEPH do	SON	do	3			do	
				GEORGE do	do	do	1			do	
				THOMAS do	BROTHER	do	18			do	
100	HINCKS YARD	1		JOSEPH COOK	HEAD	MAR	63		GENERAL LABOURER	do COVENTRY	
				MARY do	WIFE	do		65		do ATHERSTONE	
				GEORGE do	SON	UNM	22		BRICKLAYER LABOURER	do	
				THOMAS do	SON	MAR	39		HATTER do	do do	

Total of Houses: 5   Total of Males and Females: 14   7

Note – Draw your pen through such words of the headings as are inapplicable.

For more family history charts and forms, visit www.ancestry.com/save/charts/census.htm